BEST BUILDINGS
BRITAIN

LUSTER

INTRODUCTION

This is an unusual sort of guide. Rather than offering the choices of a single authority on architecture, *Best Buildings – Britain* relies on the combined efforts of 31 enquiring and idiosyncratic minds. Starting in London, the book takes you on an illustrated nationwide tour of 75 buildings completed since 1918. To arrive at this point, we invited a wide selection of architects and experts to list ten of their favourites. Those who were kind enough to respond submitted a tremendously diverse selection — some chose more than ten, some chose fewer; some even bent the rules a little. Every one of those lists is reproduced in full at the end of the book and, from all these, 75 buildings were picked for the main section.

Some choices are instantly recognisable and would rightly appear in any selection of the greatest. Certain buildings (such as the De La Warr Pavilion, the Royal Festival Hall and the Lloyd's Building) sailed through the process, coming up again and again. Similarly, a few key names (Lasdun, Lubetkin, Smithson, Stirling) featured on many lists. Alongside those, however, there are plenty of surprises.

Aside from the main 75, the lists at the back offer you the details of over 100 more buildings to rediscover, or perhaps to encounter for the first time. The choices are so varied that almost everyone will stumble upon something unfamiliar. Several have already been demolished. A few are not strictly buildings at all. At least three of them never really existed in the first place.

And even if nothing here is completely new to you, there is still the fascination of seeing who has picked what, which choices are shared, and which turn out to be lone pleasures.

Thank you to every contributor that took the trouble to agonise over a selection of buildings for this book. We hope it offers you a fresh perspective on 100 years of British architecture.

Matthew Freedman

CONTENTS

LONDON

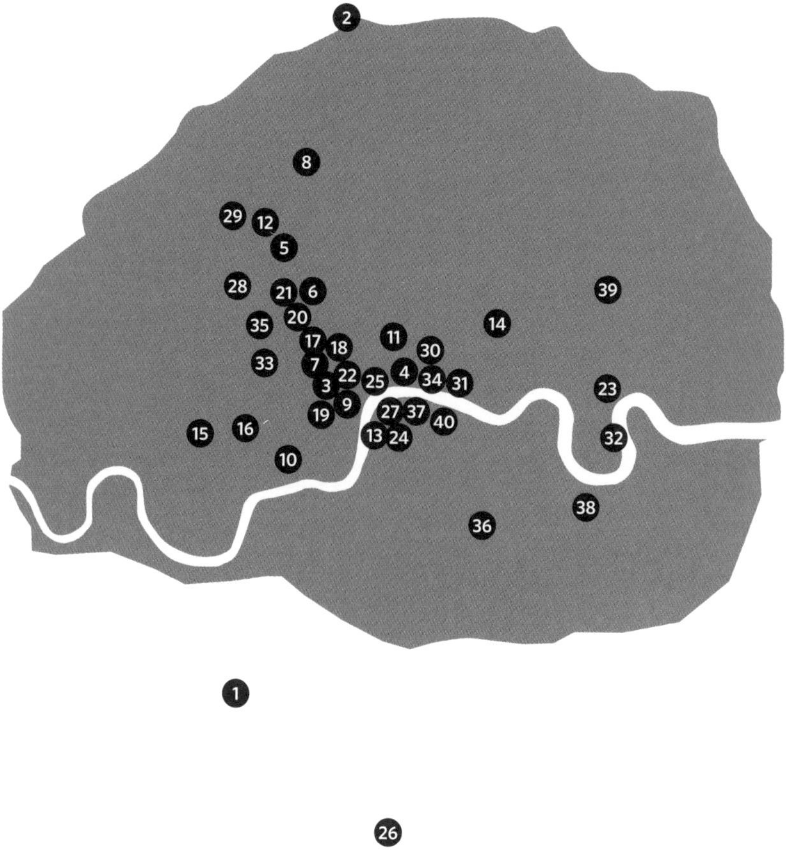

1
2
3
4
5
6
7
8
9
10
11
12
13
14
15
16
17
18
19
20
21
22
23
24
25
26
27
28
29
30
31
32
33
34
35
36
37
38
39
40

UNITED KINGDOM

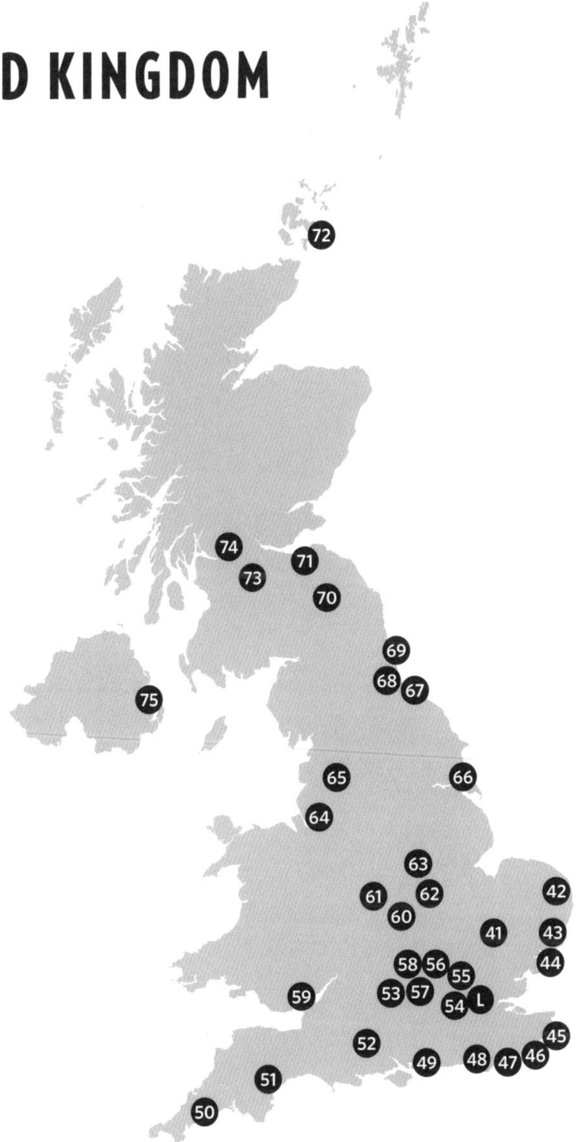

GRANADA CINEMA

TOOTING

❶ **Mitcham Road, Tooting, London SW17**
Completed in: 1931
Architect: Cecil Masey (1881-1960)

> **"Though it is not likely to evoke the enthusiasm of the architectural purist, it again stamps its sponsors as formidable exponents of modernism in the cinema field."** (Report in *The Bioscope*, 1931)

The Granada is a spectacular surviving example from an era of prolific, competitive art deco cinema-building. It owes its existence to a boom in the interwar years that saw big chains such as Odeon, Gaumont and Granada opening throughout the country. This brought new picture houses on varying scales of grandeur and whimsicality to every town. The largest seated thousands and stopped at nothing to promote themselves as a perfect escape from the daily grind. Contributors to this guide have also chosen the Odeon, Leicester Square with its tremendous black granite façade (1937), the suburban, portholed and neon-lit Odeon, Redhill (1938) and the Gaumont State Cinema (1937) on Kilburn High Road in North West London, whose 40-metre-high tower was designed to mimic the Empire State Building. Sidney Bernstein's Granada chain had a reputation for sumptuous interiors, and the Tooting outpost is an overwhelming example. The building was designed by Bernstein's long-term architect Masey, with interiors masterminded by the Russian émigré designer and theatre director, Theodore Komisarjevsky (1882-1954).

The outside is relatively restrained, with four huge Greek revival columns over the entrance canopy. But the palatial, neo-Gothic interiors are something else – from the cavernous foyer with sweeping travertine staircases to the vast auditorium, once capable of seating 4000. There is embellishment everywhere: clever paint effects, stained glass, friezes, chandeliers, hallways lined with mirrors and Gothic arches, coffered and ornamented ceilings and, of course, a Wurlitzer organ (still in place) that rises from beneath the screen. "When the lights go up there is Aladdin's cave," insisted the critic Iain Nairn in 1966. "Miss the Tower of London, if you have to, but don't miss this." As cinema attendances dropped steeply from the 1960s, the cinema hosted concerts by the Beatles and the Bee Gees among many others, and finally closed its doors in 1973. It reopened in 1976 as a bingo hall and has remained so ever since.

ARNOS GROVE UNDERGROUND STATION

2 Bowes Road, Arnos Grove, London N11
Completed in: 1932
Architect: Charles Holden (1875-1960)

London's Underground stations were powerful ambassadors of modern architecture and design in the 1930s, seen and experienced daily by millions. The restrained, functional designs and repeated use of simple geometric shapes are frequently the work of Charles Holden, in prolific collaboration with Frank Pick, the visionary senior executive at the organisation that became London Transport. Pick oversaw a corporate identity that embraced the famous house typeface (Johnston Sans), signage, map design and station architecture.

Holden's career began early in the 20th century and encompassed the design of Oscar Wilde's tomb at Père Lachaise (1912, with Jacob Epstein), many First World War cemeteries and memorials, and London landmarks including Senate House (1937) in Bloomsbury. His London Underground work hit its stride in the mid-1920s, increasingly influenced by contemporary European public architecture, and grew into a sequence of dozens of station buildings over the following decade and after the War. Many are boxy and rectangular with flat overhanging concrete canopies. Cylinders, heptagons and other bold shapes are often involved. Arnos Grove's tall, cylindrical, brick and glass ticket hall, set within a low square base, is said to have been inspired by Stockholm Public Library (1928). A key feature is the generous window space, common to most Holden stations. On the inside, the drum of the ticket hall is an impressive place; from outside, it's a reassuring sight when lit up in the evening. The station has kept plenty of original features, from the central, circular ticket booth to the platform clocks and timber benches. Arnos Grove and Southgate (next stop north on the Piccadilly Line, with its rooftop feature resembling an outsize electrical insulator) are among Holden's best work. They feel like rather English takes on modern European styles of the time: a hint of imagined futures from contemporary films like *Metropolis* and *Things to Come*, but nothing too potent for conventional tastes.

ARNOS GROVE
RVP
No parking
Offenders will be prosecuted
No parking
Offenders will be prosecuted

BROADCASTING HOUSE

3 Portland Place, London W1
Completed in: 1932
Architects: George Val Myer (1883-1959) & F. J. Watson Hart (1880-1953)

By the time the British Broadcasting Corporation moved into its first purpose-built headquarters, the listening nation was already starting to accord it mythic status. Steered by its first director-general, John Reith, the BBC was perceived by many as an unimpeachable source of news, information and entertainment. This reputation would take hold even more profoundly during wartime. The new headquarters, planned from 1928 by Myer together with the BBC's own civil engineer, Marmaduke Tudsbery Tudsbery, implied the organisation's growing stature. The steel-framed building has a long, impressive, mildly intimidating nine-storey frontage. The Portland stone and ordered arrangement of windows relate it to the London tradition of Nash's Georgian terraces in nearby Regent Street; the art deco styling and flourishes are proudly modern for the time. The resulting mix is forward-looking but sensible. Broadcasting House curves sharply round at Langham Place, and over the main entrance on this corner is Eric Gill's famous statue of Prospero and Ariel. Other reliefs by Gill, Eric Aumonier and Gilbert Bayes decorate the exterior.

The innermost parts were all about the technological needs of radio production and broadcast. At the core is a windowless brick tower, designed to insulate the studios and concert hall within from all external sound. With Raymond McGrath in charge, these spaces were planned for the latest needs of radio by several major figures of modernist design, including Serge Chermayeff and Wells Coates. Sadly, with the ever-advancing changes in broadcast technology, none of these original interiors survives. In recent times, after the closure of the Corporation's fondly-remembered Television Centre in White City, the television news service moved to Broadcasting House as part of a series of alterations that have made the complex much bigger. In 2007 a similarly shaped building by MJP Architects was added opposite the original, and the two were then linked at one end by a curved extension, making an open-air space in the middle that is often seen in television broadcasts.

DAILY EXPRESS BUILDING

4 Fleet Street, London EC4
Completed in: 1932
Architects: Ellis and Clarke & Owen Williams (1890-1969)

The Fleet Street headquarters of Lord Beaverbrook's *Daily Express* was one of a family of three similarly exciting, futuristic-looking city bases designed to project the newspaper's relevance to a modern nation. After the London building came one in Albion Street, Glasgow (1936) and a third in Ancoats, Manchester (1939). The advanced engineering was masterminded by Owen Williams, who collaborated with the practice of Ellis and Clarke in London but designed the Manchester building himself. Williams's construction system – using reinforced concrete portal frames – permitted the dark, uninterrupted, curving frontages that characterise all three buildings.

The Fleet Street HQ was a dramatic arrival in a congested location at the centre of the British press universe, among more conventional architectural neighbours. It was emblematic of the newspaper's leading-edge technology and ambitious self-image: the printing presses occupied the basement, and the seven storeys above housed all other staff behind a mysterious curtain wall of black vitrolite and chrome strips. In reference to the Soviet-era headquarters of the KGB, satirical magazine *Private Eye* christened it 'The Black Lubyanka' in the 1960s. Most of the interior spaces have been much changed, but the entrance from Fleet Street still leads to an extravagant art deco foyer by the architect Robert Atkinson (1883-1952) with a sunburst-effect ceiling, gilt pendant light and details in vitrolite, marble, rosewood and chrome. On either side are intricate reliefs depicting 'Britain' and 'Empire' by Eric Aumonier (sculptor of the huge archer (1940) on top of East Finchley underground station). In its original form, the foyer features heavily in *The Day the Earth Caught Fire* (1961), a disaster movie in which *Daily Express* journalists save humanity from "the stupid, crazy irresponsible bunglers" who have endangered the Earth by testing atomic bombs. Express Newspapers left in 1989 and the building is now used as offices, with the foyer very occasionally open to the public. John Robertson Architects completed a painstaking restoration of the building in 2000, refurbishing the outside and foyer, and remaking some details that had gone missing.

THE ISOKON BUILDING

(LAWN ROAD FLATS)

5 Lawn Road, Hampstead, London NW3
Completed in: 1934
Architect: Wells Coates (1895-1958)

Lawn Road flats, later renamed The Isokon, was built for Jack and Molly Pritchard by Wells Coates, and was one of the very first Modern Movement blocks in the country. Its reinforced concrete construction, its hypnotically fluent exterior, and the cast of intelligentsia involved in its history have made it symbolic of the social and architectural experiments of its era. Some towering avant-garde émigrés played a part in its early life: Bauhaus luminaries Walter Gropius and László Moholy-Nagy took flats here, and Marcel Breuer co-designed the ground floor residents' club, The Isobar. 1940s residents included Agatha Christie, who described it as "a giant liner which ought to have had a couple of funnels, and then you went upstairs and through the door of your flat, and there were the trees tapping on the window".

Isokon was the company formed by Jack Pritchard and Wells Coates, dedicated to progressive design in housing and furniture. Lawn Road was their first collaboration and Coates's first completed building. The concept was to provide 'minimum flats': precision-designed, modest accommodation, full of built-in features like sliding tables, doors and room dividers, and on-site services that would allow young professional residents to lead streamlined, 'modern' lives with a community dimension. The minimum flat concept is repeated across all four floors, with a penthouse on top originally occupied by the Pritchards. A promotional brochure of 1938 offers "shoe-cleaning, window-cleaning, everything done for you", with meals from the ground floor kitchens served directly to the flats. The functional, austerely utopian approach was strongly influenced by the ideas of Le Corbusier, whom Coates and Pritchard both admired. As with Embassy Court in Brighton, the other Wells Coates building featured in this book (see p. 104), The Isokon slid into severe disrepair from the 1970s onwards. The decline was arrested and reversed in the early 2000s, with an impeccable refurbishment by Avanti Architects. The Isokon Gallery, on the site of the old garage on the ground floor, tells the building's story and also has some examples of the Isokon Company's furniture on display: clever, innovative plywood pieces like the Isokon Long Chair (1937) or the Penguin Donkey, a mini bookcase. The gallery is open to the public on selected weekends.

PENGUIN POOL

LONDON ZOO

❻ **Regent's Park, London NW1**
Completed in: 1934
Architects: Tecton - Berthold Lubetkin (1901-1990)

Perhaps the most instantly engaging and famous of the three London Zoo structures in this guide (see also p. 48 and p. 50). An early project for Berthold Lubetkin and the Tecton Group, it is also a showcase for the potential of reinforced concrete in the hands of inventive experts. The cool, white oval structure, with steps and nesting boxes at the edges, houses a pool crossed by two long, cantilevered ramps that loop and overlap but never touch. This sculptural, magical-looking feat was worked out by Lubetkin in close conjunction with the structural engineers Ove Arup (1895-1988) and Felix Samuely (1902-1959). It was the debut in a series of collaborations between Lubetkin and Arup, mostly in London. These were to include the Highpoint blocks (1935 and 1938, see p. 24), Finsbury Health Centre (1938, see p. 30) and the Spa Green Estate (1949). For Lubetkin, the curving ramps were also a rehearsal for the design of the famous circular staircase landings at Bevin Court (1954), his public housing development in Islington.

The Pool – an avant-garde and theatrical attraction for zoo visitors – was a huge success, with audiences crowding around to view the penguins troop doggedly up and down their 14-metre-long ramps for many years. The experience worked for spectators and aligned with the latest animal welfare thinking of the time, but ultimately turned out less happy for the residents. Among other issues, the concrete of the poolside (originally covered with a gentler rubber surfacing) and the celebrated ramps were not kind to penguin feet. After several cases of an unpleasant infection called bumblefoot, the penguins left Lubetkin's pool in 2004 for an upgrade to Penguin Beach, elsewhere on the premises. As one of London Zoo's diverse collection of listed buildings dating from the 1820s onwards, it has been preserved intact as a quintessential modernist structure, but is currently vacant.

RIBA HEADQUARTERS

7 **Portland Place, London W1**
Completed in: 1934
Architect: George Grey Wornum (1888-1957)

When it was Grade II* listed in 1970, architect Alison Smithson apparently told the *Evening Standard* that it should be dynamited, but the dignified art deco home of the Royal Institute of British Architects survived regardless. It continues to perform its original function after 85 years: a purpose-built headquarters for the industry's professional body, with facilities open to all. The building is the best-known work of Grey Wornum, whose career was interrupted by the First World War. He lost his right eye in combat and wore a dark-tinted monocle to conceal it, as portrayed in the bronze bust set into the wall near the entrance. Wornum won RIBA's 1929 competition to design a new HQ, and completed the work in time for its centenary in 1934. The interiors were planned with his wife, artist and designer Miriam Gerstle (1898-1989).

Despite the simple, clean lines of the Portland stone-clad exterior, it's not a sparse, Corbusian building. Wornum produced a design in a mellower, Scandinavian-inflected strain of modernism, with neoclassical elements and plenty of rich, decorative detail. 66 Portland Place is packed with beautiful works extolling the architectural profession and associated skills and trades. High over the entrance is Architectural Aspiration, a relief of a giant, mythic figure reaching for the sky, by Edward Bainbridge Copnall (1903-1973). The huge bronze front doors by sculptor James Woodford (1893-1976) depict the River Thames and various notable London buildings. The central space inside is dominated by four marble pillars rising to the top of the building, along with the splendid marble staircase, bronze banisters and etched glass balustrade panels. The Henry Florence Memorial Hall on the first floor is full of reliefs, carvings and ceiling panels depicting architectural history's high points. The galleried RIBA library, with its specially designed bookcases ending in elegant curves, holds one of the world's great architectural collections, and is regularly open to the public. There is a bookshop, a café, and a regular programme of events and exhibitions. One of RIBA's past presidents, Owen Luder, gives his list of ten favourite buildings at the end of this book.

forcefully
removed
LOOK RIGHT

HIGHPOINT I & HIGHPOINT II

8 **North Hill, Highgate, London N6**
Completed in: 1935 & 1938
Architect: Tecton – Berthold Lubetkin (1901-1990)

The two Highpoint blocks owe their existence to Sigmund Gestetner's plans for an estate of high-quality subsidised housing for his workers. The Gestetner company manufactured duplicating machines in nearby Tottenham and prided itself on the welfare of its thousands of employees. The project was most suitable for Berthold Lubetkin, who had arrived in London from the Soviet Union in 1931, keen to apply his socialist principles in his architectural work. He designed Highpoint I as an H-shaped, reinforced concrete block of two- and three-bedroom flats on eight floors, supported on a series of elegant columns. It was built high on a hill in the North London village of Highgate, with views to the city, cleverly designed modern interiors, an outdoor pool and gardens. Lubetkin's interest in the forms and ideas of Le Corbusier (who visited in 1935 and declared the block "an achievement of the first rank") can be clearly seen. The smooth, white exterior, the steel-framed windows, and the famous curve of its cantilevered balconies have made the building a defining example of the modern movement in Britain. Public interest was much greater than anticipated, and most of the 60 flats were snapped up by more well-heeled tenants than Gestetner and Lubetkin had in mind.

Highpoint II (1938) is smaller, lower and more luxuriously appointed. There are just twelve apartments, some with double-height living rooms, and a penthouse at the top that was Lubetkin's. It is faced in brick and tile, rather than the white render of the earlier block. The entrance canopy is supported by two caryatids (classical Greek female figures doing service as pillars) who, strictly speaking, appear not to belong. Sometimes assumed to be a gauche, anti-modernist later addition, they were Lubetkin's own ironical, ornamental touch. They add a whimsical note to the deep elegance of the place, which has represented modernist refinement continuously from the first pioneer residents, to Emma Peel of *The Avengers* in the 1960s, to today's lucky owners.

203-206 PICCADILLY: SIMPSON'S
(NOW WATERSTONES)

9 **London W1**
Completed in 1936
Architect: Joseph Emberton (1889-1956)

Probably London's most distinctive, familiar and accessible ambassador of 1930s retail design, this shop opened to the public in 1936 as the purpose-built headquarters of Simpson's. It was the ultimate department store for the modern gentleman, offering a complete outfitting service, bespoke tailoring, haircuts, cigars, and even accessories for customers' dogs, as well as cocktails and food on the top floor. Sleek modernity, alongside the store's more staid Piccadilly neighbours, was a central aspect of its appeal. These days, a slightly time-worn landmark as well as a pioneering retail space, it is the flagship branch of Waterstones booksellers, and the largest bookshop in Europe. The architect, Joseph Emberton, was an expert creator of modernist public buildings for various uses. His other work between the Wars includes the Royal Corinthian Yacht Club in Burnham-on-Crouch (1931) and the casino at Blackpool Pleasure Beach (1940).

The steel-framed building on Piccadilly is full of clever features, novel at the time, that indicate Simpson's as a progressive force in store design. Above pavement level, expanses of Portland stone run all the way across the building, alternating with uninterrupted strips of windows. The steeply concave glazing on the ground floor lets window-shoppers enjoy the displays unhindered by distracting reflections. Inside, an immense chrome-plated light fitting suspended from the top floor extends down its entire height, at the core of a grand travertine marble staircase. Most of the six levels are designed as huge, open retail spaces, extending from Piccadilly at the front right through to Jermyn Street at the back, with natural light entering from both ends. In concert with Emberton's architectural design and fittings, a stellar cast of modernist creatives set the groundbreaking tone of the store. The key Bauhaus school figure László Moholy-Nagy designed window displays and merchandise layouts. Graphic designer Ashley Havinden shaped the house style with a suave, tubular 1930s logo, still visible on the front of the building, and matching stationery and packaging. From the 1940s, the pioneering display designer Natasha Kroll continued the innovation in Simpson's windows and in-store display. Decades later, the chic 1930s aura lingers on, and the southerly views from the fifth floor restaurant are still worth the journey to the top.

Waterstones
W
W
Waterstones
Simpson

PETER JONES

10 Sloane Square, Chelsea, London SW1
Completed in: 1937
Architects: William Crabtree (1905-1991), J.A. Slater (1885-1963), A.H. Moberly (1886-1952) & C.H. Reilly (1874-1948)

This Chelsea institution, the local department store for a perpetually prosperous bit of West London, has existed on the same site since the 19th century. But the construction of the 'real' Peter Jones, the seven-storey Modern Movement building that dominates the western end of Sloane Square today, began in 1932. It was part of a between-the-wars wave of forward-looking construction and expansion, when the department store was a central commercial force in British towns and cities. Peter Jones, like Simpson's (see p. 26), was a dramatic break with the grandiose architectural styles of stores like Harrods and Selfridges, dating from earlier in the century. Other examples include art deco giants D.H. Evans in Oxford Street and Kendal Milne in Manchester, both completed in 1936 by Harrods in-house architect Louis David Blanc (1877-1944).

The store's innovative form was a calculated move by John Spedan Lewis (creator of the John Lewis Partnership as it exists today, who bought Peter Jones in 1914) to bring shoppers to an exciting new landmark. The pioneering steel-framed structure was the first Modern Movement building in the country with a glass curtain wall. The short end faces Sloane Square, then bulges briefly as it curves around the corner and stretches down King's Road. The design has its own fluid elegance but shows the clear influence of Erich Mendelsohn's sleek, curtain-walled German stores of the mid-1920s. Mendelsohn himself was in England by this time, completing the De La Warr Pavilion in 1935 (see p. 102). Department stores are no longer the undisputed giants and innovators of retail, yet Peter Jones remains a modernist fixture in this smartest of London neighbourhoods. When its locals were expertly classified and tenderly mocked by Ann Barr and Peter York in *The Official Sloane Ranger Handbook* (1982), Peter Jones was listed as a key emporium for the purchase of "Sloaniture and Sloanishings". John McAslan and Partners finished a very extensive refurbishment in 2004, modernising the store facilities within, while leaving the famous exterior completely intact.

FINSBURY HEALTH CENTRE

⑪ Pine Street, Clerkenwell, London EC1
Completed in: 1938
Architect: Tecton - Berthold Lubetkin (1901-1990)

A landmark modernist public building, and perhaps the project that came closest to fulfilling Berthold Lubetkin's deeply held beliefs that architecture and planning must play central roles in realising a better, fairer world. Its aims aligned with the founding principles of the National Health Service in the years following the Second World War, even though Finsbury Health Centre was completed a decade before. It was visionary, in terms of its design as well as the range of health services offered under one roof. A war-time poster by Abram Games depicted the intentions and the context: the clean, white, modern marvel of Finsbury Health Centre replacing the unhygienic neglect and decay of an earlier era, underlined by the message 'YOUR BRITAIN – FIGHT FOR IT NOW'.

The building was commissioned by a London council intent on providing decent health care in a deprived inner-city area. Dr Chuni Lal Katial of the council's health committee, an immigrant from India, approached Lubetkin, an immigrant from Russia, to build a pioneering centre for local health provision free at the point of use. The design combines Lubetkin's established, socially-aware modernist approaches with a contemporary belief in the healing properties of sunlight, ventilation and fresh air. Visitors enter a central pavilion entirely fronted in glass bricks and white tile, with angled wings at either side containing the medical services and offices. The building's forms were intended to signal a welcoming embrace into a light, bright, universally accessible world of modern medical care, with radiantly coloured ceilings, walls and pillars. Vivid health-promoting murals (now lost) by designer Gordon Cullen depicted deck chairs, pot plants and calisthenics, as well as health-promoting mottoes such as 'Fresh air night and day' and 'Chest diseases are preventable and curable'. Despite enduring periods of poor maintenance and questions over its future as a health facility, Finsbury Health Centre remains publicly owned and continues to serve its original purpose for the local community.

FINSBURY

1, 2 & 3 WILLOW ROAD

⓬ **Hampstead, London NW3**
Completed in: 1939
Architect: Ernő Goldfinger (1902-1987)

Ian Fleming, Hampstead resident and creator of James Bond, was meant to have hated Ernő Goldfinger's work at Willow Road so much that he borrowed his surname for the villainous, megalomaniacal gold fetishist of his 1959 novel and 1964 film. Whatever the truth of the story, the association probably enhanced the architect's public reputation as a creator of inhospitable buildings The projects most associated with Goldfinger are indeed opinion-dividing brutalist blocks: Balfron Tower (1967, see p. 54) and Trellick Tower (1972). However, this terrace of three houses on Willow Road (overlooking Hampstead Heath) was completed decades before, in 1939. In the 1930s, Hampstead was home to an intellectual and bohemian community, including recent European émigrés such as Goldfinger himself, originally from Hungary. Willow Road was among the architect's first major projects in Britain and is a fine example of the Modern Movement housing identified with the period: flat-roofed, concrete-framed, full of space and light inside, with a sober exterior combining elements of contrast and harmony with its neighbours. Goldfinger lived in number two with his family until his death in 1987. The house is now owned by the National Trust and regularly open to the public.

From the street, the terrace is an orderly, uninterrupted frontage with generous picture windows to the living rooms on the first floor – at first sight it could be mistaken for a single, very substantial home. The use of brick (rather than the common 1930s 'moderne' finish of bright white stucco) allows the houses to blend with adjacent older buildings. Inside, number two is full of original interior features designed by the architect, from furniture, storage and children's games to sliding screens and folding doors that maximise the adaptability of the living spaces. A central staircase with an elegant, spindly banister spirals up through the whole building towards a skylight in the roof. The star-studded art collection gathered by Goldfinger and his wife Ursula Blackwell (1901-1999) is displayed throughout, including work by Blackwell herself, Henry Moore, Man Ray, Bridget Riley and many others.

ROYAL FESTIVAL HALL

⓭ **Belvedere Road, Lambeth, London SE1**
Completed in: 1951
Architects: Robert Matthew (1906-1975), Leslie Martin (1908-2000) & Peter Moro (1911-1998)

The Festival of Britain, an orchestrated moment of national pride and optimism for a post-war future, was specifically designed to exist for just a few months in 1951. Once Ralph Tubbs's Dome of Discovery, Powell & Moya's Skylon, and the other temporary structures were cleared from the south bank of the Thames, one permanent legacy remained: the Royal Festival Hall, a modernist palace built with austerity-defying materials and attention to detail. The team of London County Council architects was led by Robert Matthew, Leslie Martin and Peter Moro, and expanded to involve a wealth of young and creative talent. Moro was also the designer of the famous 'net and ball' pattern carpet used throughout the building. This was one of a series of colourful, semi-abstract graphic devices that tempered modernism with playfulness and shaped what became known as Festival Style.

At the core of the Festival Hall is the huge auditorium, supported on columns and surrounded by foyers to exclude noise and vibration from outside. Its beautiful wood panelling, seating designed by Robin and Lucienne Day, and ranks of curvy, cantilevered audience boxes are little changed. The positioning conforms to what Leslie Martin described as the "egg in the box": as well as providing sound insulation, it permits free flow of people beneath and around the auditorium, allowing for the Festival Hall's generous, open public areas. In the following decade there were modifications to the exterior surfaces and glazing, resulting in what the Historic England listing describes as a building "in the spirit of the Festival of Britain, amended in the 1960s in accordance with Corbusian loyalties". Since then, the Royal Festival Hall has become firmly rooted in the affections of most Londoners, somehow retaining its ambience of democratic accessibility in a world of increasingly privatised public space. Architects Allies and Morrison completed a major refurbishment in 2007, improving the acoustics of the auditorium and increasing the public areas. The oldest of the extended family of cultural venues on the South Bank, the Royal Festival Hall remains a modernist landmark at the centre of London's cultural life.

KEELING HOUSE

14 Claredale Street, Bethnal Green, London E2
Completed in: 1959
Architects: Denys Lasdun (1914-2001)

This was Denys Lasdun's second project for the Borough Council in the historically poor working-class district of Bethnal Green. Amid the urgent post-war need for quality home, Lasdun became dissatisfied with what he saw as the monotonous and alienating properties of much high-rise council housing. His answer was the 'cluster block': by grouping flats in several angled wings attached to a core tower that housed the lifts and services, he hoped to balance domestic privacy and community spirit in a modernist, multi-storey version of the area's older housing patterns. Accordingly, Keeling House is made up of four 16-storey towers, grouped around a central building. Blocks are angled so that all flats receive a share of sunlight through the day and – crucially – no one has an indiscreetly direct view into a neighbour's home from their balcony. As well as lifts, the core building was planned with outdoor laundry-drying areas where it was hoped the residents would socialise.

Opinions differed on whether Lasdun engineered the desired mix of privacy and community that he identified in the Victorian terraces that Keeling House replaced. Many new residents were delighted with their flats, but some observers found Lasdun's ambitions overly optimistic. Writing in 1963, the social historian Colin Ward was wary of too much nostalgia for "that horizontal matey neighbourliness which we have been taught to associate with the tight little terraces of old Bethnal Green". Without doubt, Keeling House is witness to a genuine post-war determination to offer decent council housing to British people. The building fell into disrepair in the 1970s, and Tower Hamlets Council eventually declared itself unable to fund expensive work on the reinforced concrete structure. It was reprieved from almost certain demolition when it was listed in 1993, but its future remained uncertain until 1999, when a developer bought it. The fabric of the building was carefully restored and it has a second, privatised life as luxury housing. The topmost maisonettes on each block, along with the rooftop water tower, have become penthouses, and there is a new glass-walled lobby and a water feature at the entrance.

COMMONWEALTH INSTITUTE

(NOW THE DESIGN MUSEUM)

15 **Kensington High Street, London W8**
Completed in: 1962
Architects: Robert Matthew Johnson-Marshall & Partners

The Commonwealth Institute opened in 1962 to promote a progressive, post-Empire family of nations that was better suited to the modern era than its Victorian predecessor, the Imperial Institute. It was a gentle public relations offensive that proved widely popular, and a magnet for parties of schoolchildren over many years. The building's fabric featured materials summoned from Commonwealth nations – copper donated by Zambia, timber from Nigeria, and so on. Visitors approached from Kensington High Street through an environment designed by the landscape architect Sylvia Crowe (1901-1997), which has been lost in recent changes to the site. Passing a forest of poles flying the flags of every Commonwealth country, they crossed a moat on a covered walkway to the entrance. Inside, a set of display spaces rose elegantly through three tiers, where member nations had displays depicting an authorised version of their history and culture. There was an art gallery and restaurant overlooking Holland Park and a cinema showing Commonwealth-related films. Outside and within, the star design feature was the concrete, copper-covered roof: an extraordinary, swooping 'hyperbolic paraboloid' engineering feat in the futuristic spirit of Eero Saarinen's TWA Flight Center (1962) at JFK Airport in New York.

A publicly funded exhibition space extolling the Commonwealth's virtues, the Institute built on the approach of the previous decade's Festival of Britain. But enthusiasm for the project waned over time, the building's maintenance cost magnified (mainly due to the chronically leaky roof) and it eventually closed in 2004. It sat empty and imperilled for many years, despite being listed at Grade II* in 1988, until its recent rebirth as a fresh location for the Design Museum in 2016. From its origins in the Victoria and Albert Museum, the Design Museum found a longer-term home in 1989 at Shad Thames, near Tower Bridge. By moving to the Commonwealth Institute site it has tripled its space. The celebrated roof remains, more the focal point than ever before, but with a completely new, austere interior of pale oak and marble designed by John Pawson. The gallery spaces host a permanent collection narrating modern design history and a programme of changing exhibitions.

the
DESIGN
MUSEUM

ROYAL COLLEGE OF ART

16 Kensington Gore, Kensington, London SW7
Completed in: 1963
H. T. Cadbury-Brown (1913-2009), Hugh Casson (1910-1999)
& Robert Goodden (1909-2002)

The RCA can trace its history as a school of art and design back to 1837. Today it is an institution of international stature, incubating postgraduate talent in art, architecture, fashion, product design and related fields. Under Robin Darwin, the college's visionary post-war principal, three of its eminent teaching staff planned a purpose-built home at this prominent site facing Kensington Gardens. On a lean budget, Henry Thomas 'Jim' Cadbury-Brown designed a flexible, contemporary building capable of housing facilities – from studios to looms to kilns to presses – that would revitalise British industrial design through practical study. The main block, the Darwin Building, is a sombre structure clad in dark brick. Over its eight storeys, pairs of tall, metal-framed windows with concrete mullions lend it a strong vertical emphasis.

The College shares this stretch of Kensington Gore with distinguished Victorian neighbours: the Royal Albert Hall is next door to the east; beyond that is Albert Hall Mansions. This is the northern end of Albertopolis, the zone of august cultural institutions that developed in the years after the Great Exhibition of 1851 with Prince Albert's patronage. The RCA is a much later arrival, and a striking contrast, yet Cadbury-Brown made sure that it clearly acknowledged its context. The gables at the top of Albert Hall Mansions are echoed by the set-back sections at the top of the Darwin Building, and its dark brick exterior was chosen to match the richly grimy, soot-stained surfaces of its older neighbours. These have since been dramatically deep-cleaned, making the RCA less complementary. However, even as the least Albertopolitan structure of the group overlooking Kensington Gardens and the Albert Memorial, it has aged to become an integral part of the neighbourhood. Major change loomed in the early 2000s, when plans were approved for a five-storey extension to replace the low-level Gulbenkian Wing facing the Albert Hall. Cadbury-Brown himself protested, writing in a letter to the *Architects' Journal* that it "would be a leech or louse sucking blood from a corner of the Darwin Building". The idea was abandoned, and the RCA has continued to expand elsewhere in London on its campuses at Battersea and White City.

Royal College of Art
Darwin Building

ROYAL COLLEGE OF PHYSICIANS

17 St Andrews Place, London NW1
Completed in: 1964
Architect: Denys Lasdun (1914-2001)

The Royal College of Physicians, the eminent body of medical professionals established in the early 16th century, bought the site of what was to be their new headquarters in 1958. The location on the eastern side of Regent's Park was in the sensitive context of John Nash's Regency villas and terraces. In fact, it was on the site of a severely bomb-damaged Nash house, which was then demolished so that work could begin. After reviewing a list of recommendations drawn up by John Summerson, the architectural historian and authority on Georgian London, the College made the bold choice of Denys Lasdun as their architect. Aside from the National Theatre (see p. 64), the RCP is perhaps the single building most closely identified with Lasdun. It was his most prestigious commission to date, and a key stage in the development of his rigorous, semi-abstracted, sculptural work in concrete.

The challenge was to provide a headquarters that respected the RCP's heritage and traditions, as well as providing for its modern-day functions. The building that Lasdun delivered is acknowledged as an uncompromising and elegant modern masterpiece. The entrance facing Regent's Park is blank and enigmatic, with central pillars supporting the cantilevered levels of the library above, and a few narrow, vertical window strips. It transmits a powerful mystique well-suited to a venerable institution. The exterior is clad in light grey porcelain mosaic, with dark engineering brick on the ground floor. Lasdun's own verdict was that it "accorded with the Nash terraces without imitating them". Inside, the defining feature is a pinnacle of 1960s late-modernist elegance: the full-height central hall, magnificently dominated by the broad, graceful staircase that rises in turns to the gallery above. The building accommodates the College's daily business, its libraries and unique historical collections, and even the original 17th-century interior of the Censors' Room, ingeniously transplanted from the previous headquarters to a cube emerging from the south side. Over 50 years after its completion, the premises is still occupied and maintained with pride by those for whom it was purpose-built – the clearest possible testament to its quality and functionality.

POST OFFICE TOWER

18 Cleveland Street, London W1
Completed in: 1964
Architects: Ministry of Public Building and Works - Eric Bedford (1909-2001)

> **"A triumph of modern architecture and engineering, a unique structure in which more than 13,000 tons of steel, concrete and glass have been shaped to meet the needs of progress."** (Commemorative brochure, 1966)

The Tower (now called BT Tower but widely known by its original name) was Britain's tallest building when it was completed, with the purpose of securing and revolutionising the country's telecommunications. Its inception and construction by the government was a matter of national pride. The chief function was (and remains) completely technical, but it incorporated access for a curious and mostly admiring public right from the start. It was officially opened in May 1966 by Tony Benn, Postmaster General, and Billy Butlin, whose company operated the revolving restaurant on the 34th floor. Rising from a reinforced concrete base, the Tower takes the form of an immense, hollow shaft, from which each floor of the building is cantilevered. Above the 16 storeys of technical equipment were the V-shaped microwave aerials (now replaced with satellite dishes), sited high enough to transmit telephone calls from central London to towers elsewhere in the country without obstruction. At the top, with spectacular views across London and beyond, were the public viewing levels accessed by two high-speed lifts.

The building became a wildly popular visitor attraction, as did the Top of the Tower restaurant, which revolved 360 degrees in 22 minutes and presented diners with a Certificate of Orbit at the end of their meal. The Tower has guest-starred in film and television ever since its construction began, often symbolising a bold, if uncertain, technological future. In the closing sequence of *Smashing Time* (1967), Rita Tushingham breaks into the control room and makes the revolving restaurant spin so fast that it triggers a power outage across the whole of Swinging London. After the explosion of a terrorist bomb on the 33rd floor in 1971, claimed by both the Angry Brigade and the IRA, public access was steadily reduced. The restaurant finally closed in 1980, although there are occasional hopeful rumours of its revival. Nevertheless, the Post Office Tower remains a slender, futuristic landmark that suffers less anti-modern criticism than any of its 1960s contemporaries.

with water

ECONOMIST PLAZA

19 St. James's Street, London SW1
Completed in: 1964
Architect: Alison Smithson (1928-1993) & Peter Smithson (1923-2003)

The output of Alison and Peter Smithson turns up a lot in the choices of contributors to this guide: four different works feature in the lists, and the Economist Plaza was picked seven times. It testifies to the enduring influence of their ideas, their writing, and the small number of buildings that they completed. The 1960s development for *The Economist* magazine is in St James's, a particularly smart area of London populated by 18th- and 19th-century buildings, and was commissioned to contrast very clearly (but not aggressively) with its surroundings. Boodle's, the venerable gentlemen's club, has been next door since 1782. The complex consists of three separate buildings of different heights (originally a bank, a residential block and 16 floors of Economist Group offices) arranged on a raised podium. In between there is open public space, designed as a zone of calm adjacent to the constant rush of Piccadilly. All the buildings are made of reinforced concrete clad in pitted Portland stone, with the same distinctive bevelled corners.

The Smithsons are often associated with the stark, confrontational forms of brutalism, but here the Portland stone tempers the mood, relating the building to its older neighbours. All the same, the Economist Plaza proved irresistible to film-makers keen to signal the bleak, alienating, corporate side of the 1960s. It features as a playground for a strange, rowdy mime troupe in Michelangelo Antonioni's *Blow Up* (1966). In Michael Winner's *I'll Never Forget What's'isname* (1967), company man Oliver Reed arrives at his office in the Economist Building, destroys his desk with an axe, and attempts to walk out on the rat race forever. *The Economist* sold up in 2016 and the listed development lives on, quietly refurbished and renamed Smithson Plaza, with a new café and an art gallery.

ELEPHANT & RHINOCEROS PAVILION – LONDON ZOO

20 **Regent's Park, London NW1**
Completed in: 1965
Architects: Casson Conder & Partners

This is the brutalist entrant among the three London Zoo structures in this book. Hugh Casson (having served as Director of Architecture for the Festival of Britain) was involved in overseeing a new design plan for the Zoo from the late 1950s, and this was his own contribution. Casson (1910-1999) is more often praised for his elegant architectural drawings and his talents as a manager and a fixer than as a working architect, but he was closely involved in the detail of this project, now known as the Casson Pavilion. The rough, ribbed, pick-hammered concrete of the exterior and its hulking, curved forms are deliberately conceived to make you think of the creatures they were designed to house. Each section is topped by a tapering roof covered in weathered copper. From a distance, it's possible to see the whole structure as a group of immense, thick-hided elephants gathered around a central watering hole, ignoring any spectators. Peter Guillery called the approach "zoomorphic new brutalism" in his study of the Zoo's buildings. It certainly embraces a spirit of whimsical mimicry not much associated with brutalism's priorities.

Behind the concrete of the Pavilion is a layer of brick – it was important that the building was robust enough to withstand the inevitable stresses and strains of housing elephants and rhinos. Inside, the series of circular pens that housed them is gently top-lit from the roofs, and the public follow a viewing path that snakes through the middle of the building. As society's expectations of zoos shifts and expert knowledge of animal behaviour advances, London Zoo's historical willingness to experiment with architecture has left it with a selection of notable buildings that no longer suit their intended purpose. As with Tecton's Penguin Pool and the Snowdon Aviary (1934 and 1965, both also chosen for this guide, see p. 20 and p. 50) the original tenants have been moved on to less theatrical accommodation, with the elephants now roaming in far more open spaces at Whipsnade Zoo in Bedfordshire.

SNOWDON AVIARY

LONDON ZOO

21 **Regent's Park, London NW1**
Completed in: 1965
Architects: Cedric Price (1934-2003), Frank Newby (1926-2001) & Lord Snowdon (1930-2017)

London Zoo has a distinguished history of commissioning new buildings. Its diverse estate includes Berthold Lubetkin's Penguin Pool (1934, see p. 20) and Hugh Casson's brutalist Elephant House (1965, see p. 48). All the same, the Snowdon Aviary was a daring departure, representing the coming together of several innovative minds in a moment of 1960s experimentalism in form and technology. The Zoological Society of London approached Antony Armstrong-Jones (Lord Snowdon) to develop an outline design. By this time he was already well known as a versatile photographer, and recently married to Princess Margaret. His choice of architect was Cedric Price, a dandified, provocative figure whose experimental ideas and teaching remain potent today. As plans for the Aviary were developing, Price was also working on the concept of the Fun Palace with theatre director Joan Littlewood. This was to be a modular, endlessly flexible, steel-framed "short-term plaything" given over to the democratic enjoyment of culture by all.

As with many Price projects, the Fun Palace was unrealised but highly influential. The Aviary, on the other hand, did open to the public; it was completed in 1965 after five years of planning, construction and testing with structural engineer Frank Newby. Alongside the Regent's Canal at the northern end of Regent's Park, it has the air of an art installation as much as a functional structure. Using a suspended concrete walkway, visitors share a large uninterrupted space where birds fly, perch and nest. It's a contained environment that retains a clear connection to the outdoors. Or, in the words of a Pathé news report on its opening: "a whopping great bird cage for the London Zoo". The Aviary is a 'tensegrity' structure, relying for strength on its external web of tensed steel cables and aluminium netting, stretched over a frame of steel tubes and pyramidal forms. The structure draws on the approaches of Buckminster Fuller, the American architect and theorist well known for his futuristic geodesic domes, with whom Cedric Price had collaborated before. Plans to refurbish the Aviary are being developed by the practice of another friend and admirer of Fuller, Norman Foster.

CENTRE POINT

22 **New Oxford Street, London WC1**
Completed in: 1966
Architects: Richard Seifert (1910-2001) & George Marsh (1921-1998)

> **"With Britain's entry into the E.E.C., Centre Point offers an unrivalled opportunity to organisations with imagination to occupy this spectacular office complex as their London or European Headquarters."** (Advertisement in *The Times*, 1972)

Owing to reluctance of its developer, Harry Hyams (1928-2015), to compromise on the rent or to allow more than one tenant to share it, Centre Point stayed unoccupied well into the 1970s. Regardless, its slim, sparkling white profile was admired by many as soon as it was finished in 1966. Richard Seifert's most famous building was synonymous with the youthful modernity of Swinging London. Ernő Goldfinger called it the "Pop Art skyscraper", while Nikolaus Pevsner, writing in 1973, judged it "coarse in the extreme".

Centre Point towers over the junction between Oxford Street, Tottenham Court Road and Charing Cross Road, sharing key design features with its rounder and much smaller sibling, Space House (see p. 58). George Marsh used the same system of uniform precast concrete parts to create a futuristic, hypnotically repetitive exterior over 34 slender storeys, sitting on 8 distinctively angled columns. As with Space House, the novel construction method meant that virtually no scaffolding was required on a site with little spare space available. The external structure went up at the rate of a floor a week. Another feature Centre Point shared with Space House was long-term, high-profile emptiness. While Hyams waited out the 1970s in search of a sole commercial tenant to take the entire building, London suffered an acute housing shortage, and the development's celebrity status began to work against it. It became the focus of angry protest, leading directly to the founding (and naming) of the homelessness charity, Centrepoint, in 1969. It wasn't until the 1980s that it started to approach decent levels of occupancy. In recent years the surrounding area has again undergone immense redevelopment and Centre Point, in a turnaround of usage that might astonish its developer, has been completely refurbished and converted into luxury apartments. At ground level, sadly, the original water fountains by Jupp Dernbach-Mayen have been taken away. However, they have found a new home in the woods of Hooke Park, the Architectural Association's rural campus in Dorset.

BALFRON TOWER

23 St Leonards Road, Poplar, London E14
Completed in: 1967
Architect: Ernő Goldfinger (1902-1987)

The unmistakeable outline of Balfron Tower, the 26-storey brutalist block near the Blackwall Tunnel in Poplar, East London, has become an ambassador for the strength and purity of modernist building design, widely available on mugs and tea towels. It was part of a large-scale public housing programme in a working-class district that was heavily bombed during the Blitz. The design enacted convictions that Goldfinger and his contemporaries derived from Le Corbusier: quality public housing and community spirit in cities could be replicated, and even enhanced, in the intelligent layouts of modern high-rise living. Balfron Tower comprises two connected structures: a main block of flats and maisonettes is linked to a slim service tower by walkways extending from every third floor. The service tower houses lifts and stairs, and was designed by Goldfinger to include a launderette and several social spaces for residents, including a "jazz/pop room" and a "hobby room". Its distinctive groups of narrow vertical windows contrast with the horizontal emphasis of the main block. Flats are spacious and thoughtfully laid out, materials are durable and high-quality. Hardwoods, tile and marble were used in public areas, with a bush-hammered concrete finish on much of the outside.

In March 1968, along with the first wave of council tenants, Goldfinger and his wife Ursula moved into a top floor flat at Balfron Tower. They remained for a month, chatting to residents about their experience of the new building and noting problems. The stay is framed as evidence of the architect's eagerness for feedback, or proof of his eye for a PR-stunt, according to taste. Goldfinger wrote in a letter: "Of course, there are some teething troubles ... Most of them just love the flats ... I feel rather reluctant to leave ... and return to my own house in Hampstead." Most residents were indeed positive about their new homes. But after a long period of inadequate maintenance, Balfron Tower is now in private hands and all social housing tenants have been permanently moved elsewhere. Its restoration and redevelopment as luxury housing has been controversial but is now complete. By contrast, Goldfinger's nearby Glenkerry House (1975) has remained as social housing, becoming a co-operative in 1980.

30

HAYWARD GALLERY, PURCELL ROOM & QUEEN ELIZABETH HALL

24 Southbank Centre, Belvedere Road, Lambeth, London SE1
Completed in: 1968
Architects: Greater London Council Architects Department

The Southbank Centre's main gallery for temporary exhibitions opened in July 1968, the year after the first concerts in the Queen Elizabeth Hall and Purcell Room. Together they comprise this unapologetically concrete group on the Thames, connected by walkways above ground level to their next-door neighbour from an only slightly earlier era of modernism, the Royal Festival Hall (see p. 34). Plans for the development began in the early 1960s with a team including Ron Herron, Warren Chalk and Dennis Crompton of the avant-garde collective Archigram. The complex exterior of angular concrete shapes and terraces has never united public taste, and opinions still range from antipathy through bafflement to adoration. Bare external finishes and an almost secretive approach to the Hayward Gallery offer a deliberate feel of fortification, but also invite exploration, and the buildings keep evolving. Since the 1970s the undercroft below the Queen Elizabeth Hall has taken on an unofficial life as a skate space. It is now a fixture, having defied threats of closure in recent years. In 2011 the Queen Elizabeth Hall Roof Garden was planted in collaboration with the Eden Project, enticing more visitors up from the riverside walk.

The Hayward addressed its own polarising aesthetic head-on for its 40th anniversary show, *Psycho Buildings*, which challenged artists to test its limits as an exhibition space. Accordingly, the Austrian art collective Gelitin filled a roof terrace with water and turned it into a popular boating lake. Feilden Clegg Bradley Studios recently completed a fastidious renovation, decluttering and enhancing the QEH's auditorium and idiosyncratic foyer, and returning clarity to all the public spaces in the spirit of the original plan. After years of being a central feature of the outside view, but virtually concealed from inside, the Hayward's 66 pyramidal rooflights were upgraded to admit natural light to the upper gallery as originally intended. By contrast with a history of more drastic modification proposals that never came to pass, the recent work allows a new audience to enjoy the original audacity of these buildings, which have still not been granted the protection of listing.

1 KEMBLE STREET (SPACE HOUSE)

25 **London WC2**
Completed in: 1968
Architects: Richard Seifert (1910-2001) & George Marsh (1921-1998)

Space House was completed two years after its close design relative, Centre Point (see p. 52). Both are the products of Richard Seifert's rewarding relationship with the speculative property developer, Harry Hyams, in a period of intense commercial redevelopment in London and other British cities. With their elegant, futuristic forms and details, the buildings represent perhaps the most digestible version of brutalism for many people, blended with a little op-art flair. Seifert generated work nationwide, thanks to his talent for working in concert with developers to surmount planning challenges, and his practice's adventurous contemporary designs. As well as Space House and Centre Point, other Seifert projects of the time include Tolworth Tower in South West London (1963), Gateway House in Manchester (1969), the NLA Tower in Croydon (1970, see p. 60) and Birmingham's Alpha Tower (1972).

The Space House development comprises two blocks linked by a raised walkway, but the attention grabber is the main, 16-storey, cylindrical building, sitting on a ring of striking angular supports. The lead architect, George Marsh, was the key design figure at Seifert's practice throughout the 1960s. Here, Marsh used the same patterns of cross-shaped concrete blocks and deep-set windows as at Centre Point, yet the drum shape of Space House enhances the dramatic effect even more, suggesting natural forms like honeycombs and insects' compound eyes. The approach also made sense practically and economically: using precast concrete components assembled on site meant that the building went up quickly and without the need for scaffolding. Hyams was notoriously happy to leave his new developments unoccupied while rental values rose, in search of a single corporate tenant for an entire building. In 1975, after years of emptiness, the Civil Aviation Authority moved in and, along with other government offices, have remained there ever since.

NLA TOWER

26 Addiscombe Road, Croydon, Greater London
Completed in: 1970
Architects: Richard Seifert (1910-2001) & Partners

Since 2008, Richard Seifert's 24-floor suburban skyscraper has been officially known as No. 1 Croydon; it's possible that this alludes to the Duke of Wellington's palatial Apsley House (1778) on Hyde Park Corner, often referred to as No. 1 London. The parallel is not precise, but it's certainly true that the graceful white block is among the first sights from the train window as you pull into East Croydon station. Over the years, NLA Tower, as it was originally known (it was built for Noble Lowndes Annuities), has gone by several affectionate nicknames: The Wedding Cake, The Threepenny Bit, The 50p Building. As with Centre Point and Space House in the same period (see p. 52 and 58), it's a showcase for the arresting geometric games that Seifert played with otherwise-conventional office blocks. Emerging on angled pilotis from its own roundabout next to the station, it's a stack of eight-sided storeys in alternate alignment that seem to interlock and turn as they rise. Even in a place as full of tall buildings as Croydon, it remains an exciting, singular landmark.

Croydon had a long history as a prosperous Surrey town a few miles south of London, but it underwent a turbo-charged period of redevelopment from the mid-1960s to the mid-1970s. This was partly driven by the government's decision to restrict big new commercial builds in central London, which allowed Croydon to present itself as an ideal alternative. The resulting growth was somewhat haphazard, and heavily skewed to the needs of business and car travel. But it did leave a legacy of several fine modern buildings, which are increasingly admired as today's Croydon endures a new wave of redevelopment and, hopefully, a renaissance. There is an earlier Seifert block nearby, Corinthian House (1965). To the south, Leon House (Tribich, Liefer & Starkin, 1969) has recently been converted from offices to flats, with its stunning, neo-megalithic concrete reliefs by sculptor William Mitchell uncovered after decades. A few minutes' walk from NLA Tower is the town's venerable entertainment venue, Fairfield Halls (Robert Atkinson & Partners, 1962). After a three-year closure for major refurbishment by MICA Architects, it reopened in 2019.

NATIONAL THEATRE

27 Upper Ground, Lambeth, London SE1
Completed in: 1976
Architect: Denys Lasdun (1914-2001)

The idea of establishing a publicly-funded national theatre originated in the mid-19th century but wasn't realised until 1963, under the directorship of Laurence Olivier. Its 'temporary' base for 13 years was the Old Vic Theatre near Waterloo Station, but the intention was always to give it a permanent, purpose-built home. Lasdun originally designed two complementary venues, a National Theatre and a National Opera House, that would have faced each other at a different South Bank site on the other side of the Festival Hall. In the end, a long drawn-out process of negotiation, planning and construction stretched from the 1960s into the 1970s, and resulted in a single building next to Waterloo Bridge. The company moved in, led by Peter Hall, in 1976.

This commanding, mildly mysterious structure is widely thought of as Denys Lasdun's mature masterpiece. For many, whether devotees or detractors, it is the definitive brutalist building. The crisp angles and unadorned concrete of the exterior, with its extraordinary horizontal landscape of terraces and deeply set back windows, punctuated by the huge fly towers of the theatres within, make it a unique London presence. There are three varied and versatile theatres: the fan-shaped Olivier with its immense drum-revolve, the proscenium-style Lyttelton and the smaller, flexible Cottesloe (renamed the Dorfman after recent refurbishment). The other, freely accessible spaces in this generous public building contribute just as much to its reputation and appeal. The cavernous yet intimately lit foyers and stairways may be the ultimate London venue for discerning admirers of concrete. The highly textured, board-marked surfaces of the walls change at every vantage point, contrasting with the super-smooth finish of the deeply coffered ceilings. It's an amazing display of the contractors' skills and the precise vision of the architect – and a refutation of the cliché that concrete is a harsh and unnatural medium. Haworth Tompkins completed an eight-year refurbishment and expansion in 2015, opening up more public space onto the increasingly busy riverside, while retaining an air of intimacy and expectation in the foyers.

The
VINE BOX

ALEXANDRA & AINSWORTH ESTATE

28 Camden, London NW8
Completed in: 1978
Architect: Neave Brown (1929-2018)

"I didn't think I was designing social housing, but just housing. Good London housing." (Neave Brown in *The Guardian*, 2017)

Neave Brown's work in Britain comprises three housing developments, all located in the London borough of Camden: a terrace in Winscombe Street, Highgate New Town (1965), the Dunboyne Road Estate (1977) and the Alexandra & Ainsworth Estate (1978). Forty years after all this was complete, Brown received the RIBA gold medal at the age of 88, chiefly in recognition of this period of pioneering commitment to public housing.

In contrast to the prevailing approach of the time, and to earlier blocks elsewhere on the estate, Brown's Alexandra & Ainsworth project is a low-rise development of terraced homes. Rowley Way, the key feature, is a pedestrian street paved in red brick, lined with rising, stepped-back terraces in a striking ziggurat style. Everything follows the gentle curve of the railway line that borders the estate to the north. Each home faces the traffic-free street; all, despite the density of the development, have private outside space. Indoors, carefully considered layouts with sliding partitions promote an open-plan, adaptable approach to domestic life. The sparse, austere tone of Rowley Way in photographs taken soon after its completion, has mellowed considerably since. The extensive planting has matured, and is integral to the estate's look and feel, in combination with the board-marked concrete of its construction. In the ten years between conception and completion in 1978, government attitudes to public housing changed dramatically. Sydney Cook, Camden's borough architect from 1965-73, was a progressive force for quality public housing, employing architects like Neave Brown and Peter Tábori to build homes for all parts of the local community. As government enthusiasm for that approach waned, funding shortfalls and poor maintenance led to a period of decline and difficult times for residents of the Alexandra & Ainsworth Estate. More recently, dedicated community action brought about change for the better. The estate has been listed at Grade II* since 1993, and while opinions on its aesthetic appeal still vary widely, its status as a beacon of Britain's most optimistic era of public housing provision is beyond question.

BRANCH HILL ESTATE

29 Spedan Close, Hampstead, London NW3
Completed in: 1978
Architects: Gordon Benson & Alan Forsyth

Gordon Benson and Alan Forsyth were part of the mould-breaking group of architects assembled by Sydney Cook during his tenure as Camden's borough architect from 1965 to 1973. Challenging the dominant approach of the time to council housing, they favoured low-rise developments that sought to deliver the required density of homes without building high. Both Benson and Forsyth had worked with Neave Brown on Camden's Alexandra & Ainsworth Estate (see p. 64) some years earlier. Their other public housing for Camden includes developments at Mansfield Road (1980) and Maiden Lane (1982); more recent public work includes the Museum of Scotland building in Edinburgh (1998) and the Millennium Wing of the National Gallery of Ireland (2002).

The Branch Hill Estate was built on land bought by the Council specifically for the purpose, in a well-to-do part of London at the edge of Hampstead Heath. The secluded, almost secretive, wooded location is the site of two blocks, each with three rows of stepped terraces on a sloping site. There are 21 two-storey houses in all, criss-crossed by a grid of pathways, with a clever and perhaps eccentric layout particular to its location. Exploiting the downhill nature of the site, each house has a full, topsoiled garden located on the flat roof of the house in front, which you can reach from the main rooms by a small bridge or from below by a spiral stair. The red brick paths, window shapes, plain white surfaces, and bare concrete of the exposed structure are all familiar from other Camden estates such as Alexandra Road, as is the mature greenery. Branch Hill Estate was very expensive to build. The initial price of the land, combined with the complexities of the plan and the harsh economic context of the 1970s, led to escalating costs and made the estate – pointedly located in an affluent area by a Labour council committed to public housing – a cause célèbre in the press by the time the first council tenants moved in. It remains intact and well-preserved today, albeit with most houses now privately owned.

BARBICAN COMPLEX

30 London EC2
Completed in: 1982
Architects: Chamberlin, Powell and Bon

Probably the most cohesive and best-maintained brutalist development in the country, with residents universally envied by concrete lovers, the Barbican is a huge, gracefully ageing modernist estate that has been decades in the making. Conceived in the mid-1950s and completed in the early 1980s, it still manages to feel like one coherent project, and remains somewhat impenetrable to outsiders. The first residents arrived in 1969, moving into the newly completed, low-rise terrace block, Speed House. In total there are over 2000 homes conforming to 140 carefully specified different plans, embracing flats of various sizes, penthouses, and maisonettes. The most immediately recognisable Barbican forms are perhaps the three immense triangular blocks (Cromwell Tower, Lauderdale Tower and Shakespeare Tower), each over 40 storeys high, with weathered, upward-curving concrete balconies. The complete separation of pedestrians from traffic, the vistas of painstakingly pick-hammered concrete, brown brick and tile, placid lakes and mature greenery, create an aesthetic verging on the utopian.

The Estate was built by the Corporation of the City of London on land devastated by wartime bombing, with the explicit intention of making a sparsely populated central London area residential once again. Chamberlin, Powell and Bon completed the adjacent Golden Lane Estate in 1962 and began planning the Barbican as early as 1955. The envisioned tenants were well-to-do city workers able to pay market rents, rather than those in immediate housing need – very unusual for a post-war public housing development. All homes were constructed to extremely high standards with many specially designed fittings. Today, flats with original internal features, from bespoke joinery and door furniture to Brooke Marine kitchens and Garchey waste disposal systems, are increasingly rare. The Arts Centre was the last phase to be completed, opening in 1982. It gave the Barbican a truly public dimension, providing an art gallery, a library, a concert hall with seating designed by Robin Day, theatres and cinemas. These public areas have clung to a degree of tranquility that is in shorter supply at London's other concrete culture zone, the South Bank.

LLOYD'S BUILDING

31 Lime Street, London EC3
Completed in: 1986
Architects: Richard Rogers Partnership

The new headquarters for the international insurance market, Lloyd's of London, opened in May 1986 after eight years of planning and construction. This thought-provoking and disruptive building is considered a definitive example of the high-tech style, and of 'bowellism' (although architects are understandably reluctant to be stuck with such terms). It quickly became one of the world's most instantly recognisable modern structures, was Grade I listed in 2011 at the age of 25, and is the most frequently chosen building by contributors to this book. Richard Rogers won the commission with a radical strategy that promised flexibility above all else. Developing ideas proven in earlier projects such as the Centre Pompidou (1977), it involved transferring most of the things that make buildings work – such as stairways, pipework, lavatories and lifts – to the perimeter, reserving the interior purely for the needs of the business, with floors of open, reconfigurable space. Crucially for Lloyd's, this permitted a trading floor ('The Room') and other areas that could expand or shrink, according to need.

From the outside, the effect is theatrical and futuristic: a visible inner building girded by six shiny stainless steel service towers, with permanently resident blue cranes on top for maintenance. Within, the heart of the building is the exhilarating 60-metre-high glazed atrium with its prominent concrete columns, surrounded by 16 levels of galleries. Glass-sided escalators with their works on show serve the first four floors. The design refers to Victorian engineering feats such as the ornate glazed roof of neighbouring Leadenhall Market, and also to the avant-garde imaginings of Archigram – the 1960s collective who posited Plug-in Cities and Capsule Homes with components that could be discarded, rearranged, or replaced. The building became an ambassador for the thrusting international profile of the City of London as a financial centre in the 1980s, bringing an unaccustomed touch of ultra-modern cool to the image of Lloyd's. But it was also flexible enough to incorporate continuity and tradition, reinstalling the 18th-century Robert Adam boardroom from the old offices, and returning the famous Lutine Bell to the new trading floor.

PUMPING STATION ISLE OF DOGS

32 Stewart Street, Isle of Dogs, London E14
Completed in: 1988
Architect: John Outram

John Outram's water pumping station is among a small but growing selection of postmodern buildings – colourful, metaphorical, unafraid of ornamentation and historical allusion – to have been awarded the protection of listing by Historic England since 2016. Others include China Wharf (1983) in Southwark by Piers Gough, Truro Crown Courts (1988) by Evans and Shalev, Outram's Judge Business School (1995) in Cambridge, and James Stirling's No. 1 Poultry (1998, see p. 76). The listings were a timely step: several important examples had already been demolished, and postmodernism probably remains behind brutalism in the queue of architectural styles awaiting a widespread revival of public interest. Outram dubbed his building 'The Temple of Storms', and has written detailed accounts of his diverse influences and strategies. When the Grade II* listing was awarded in 2017, he commented: "My work has been a rebellion. I refused to live in a city designed by proudly subliterate haptics whose ambition was to reduce it to mere 'plant'."

Among many other references, classical and otherwise, the entrances at both ends of the building are bordered by two very thick brick columns with complex, multi-coloured capitals in the manner of ancient Egypt, topped by a huge aircraft-style turbofan. It's an exuberant approach to the basic function of pumping storm water, looking back to an era of even more lavish buildings designed for similar functions. A key example is Joseph Bazalgette's nearby Abbey Mills Pumping Station (1868, nicknamed 'The Cathedral of Sewage'). The need for new water treatment facilities arose in the 1980s, as this area of East London was dramatically redeveloped for commercial projects such as Canary Wharf, adjacent to the Isle of Dogs. In an enterprising and enlightened move, the London Docklands Development Corporation commissioned eminent architects to produce the structures housing these services. As well as Outram's work, there were pumping stations by the Richard Rogers Partnership (1988) in Canning Town, and by Grimshaw Architects (1997) in North Woolwich.

LISSON GALLERY

33 Bell Street, Marylebone, London NW1
Completed in: 1992
Architects: Tony Fretton Architects

Nicholas Logsdail started Lisson Gallery in 1967 at the age of 21. Over more than 50 years, it has become an influential presence in the contemporary art world, with outposts in New York and Shanghai, and its roster of artists continues to grow. The gallery has introduced audiences to the work of Derek Jarman, Yoko Ono, Sol LeWitt, Carl Andre, Marina Abramović, Ai Weiwei and many others. It hosted Anish Kapoor's début exhibition in 1982. Lisson Gallery was a major early commission and ongoing project for Tony Fretton, who founded his practice in 1982. Later cultural work has included the Quay Arts Centre conversion in Newport on the Isle of Wight (1998), the refurbished and extended Camden Arts Centre (2004) and Fuglsang Art Gallery (2008) on the Danish island of Lolland. In Chelsea, he designed The Red House (2001), a sumptuous yet restrained private home fronted in red limestone, and a house for Lisson Gallery regular, Anish Kapoor, in 2008.

The gallery's main location in Marylebone comprises two connected parts: a modest Victorian former shop premises in Lisson Street, converted and greatly extended by Fretton in 1986, and a purpose-built space around the corner in Bell Street. The latter opened in 1992 to mark the gallery's 25th anniversary. Both buildings have their own entrances, connecting with each other behind the scenes to make an L-shaped network of gallery space and offices. The 1992 building exists in quiet contrast with its mostly 19th-century neighbours, in an area that is not especially arty – neither a traditional nor an alternative London gallery district. The display spaces on its ground and first floors are completely faced in glass from floor to ceiling, deliberately framing the outside views for gallery visitors within. For passers-by, the ground floor gallery is set slightly lower than street level so that, in Tony Fretton's words, "people from the neighbourhood have the advantage". This thoughtful, subtle approach positions the usual white spaces of the expensive private art gallery within an established locality, without the compulsion to make an attention-grabbing architectural statement.

NO. 1 POULTRY

34 **London EC2**
Completed in: 1997
Architects: James Stirling (1926-1992) & Michael Wilford

As James Stirling was designing this building in the 1980s, the playful, historically literate, sometimes brash aesthetics of postmodernism were in vogue. But the construction of the architect's final project didn't take place until 1994-1997, some years after Stirling's death at the age of 66. No. 1 Poultry therefore missed the high point of postmodern architecture's popularity and visibility in Britain, yet its reassessment has been slowly gathering speed ever since. The outside is a striking sequence of different geometrical forms, all clad in stripy pink and pale brown sandstone, with covered colonnades. A public route through the building crosses the spectacular atrium area from one side to the other. Above the ground floor shops are several storeys of offices, with a restaurant and landscaped roof gardens at the top. The two sides of the building converge in a point, including a cylindrical tower with a see-through clock that is often likened to the bow of an advancing ship – a comparison more often used of 1930s art deco buildings. Everywhere there are fascinating details in carefully chosen materials. The triangular atrium features deep blue ceramic tiles, multi-coloured window surrounds in tones verging on Day-Glo, granite floors and glass-walled lifts. The overall effect is confrontationally whimsical, yet also feels permanent, solid and thoughtful.

The prominent location in the city of London was inevitably sensitive because of its surroundings and its own past. The site's developer, Peter Palumbo, had commissioned a drastically different project in the late 1960s: a plaza and glass-clad tower by modernist pioneer Ludwig Mies van der Rohe. This was ruled out by the loud intervention of Prince Charles, among others. With the appointment of Stirling and Wilford, Palumbo developed something that (while no more pleasing to Prince Charles) is uniquely rooted in its location, through creative allusions to nearby buildings and to its own past. Close neighbours include Lutyens's Midland Bank building (1924) and Hawksmoor's Saint Mary Woolnoth church (1727). The site of 1 Poultry itself had been occupied by John Belcher's much-admired Mappin and Webb building of 1870, with its neo-Gothic, cone-roofed tower. James Stirling's building remains an affront to some but, having been Grade II* listed in 2016, is likely to survive for new generations of enlightened admirers.

LORD'S MEDIA CENTRE

35 Lord's Cricket Ground, St John's Wood Rd, London NW8
Completed in: 1999
Architects: Future Systems

The Marylebone Cricket Club played its first match on the present site of Lord's in 1814, but one of its landmarks, seen around the world whenever cricket is broadcast from here, is definitively 20th-century. The media centre at the world's most venerable cricket ground appears to hover benignly over proceedings at the Nursery End, opposite the famous pavilion. It comprises two levels: journalists below, broadcasters (including the BBC's Test Match Special team) above. The mysterious, smoothly curved structure, a little reminiscent of an insect's eye, is fronted with glass angled to avoid disruptive reflections for those within and without, whether spectators or players. It sits on two concrete lift shafts, one at each side, with no other support from the ground. The building itself was assembled in a Cornish shipyard and brought to London in prefabricated sections. It owes its design and construction to transport technology: it's a 'semi-monococque'. This is an aluminium shell reinforced with supports welded on to its surface – technology conventionally associated with ships' hulls, aeroplanes and car bodies, rather than cricket grounds.

The strange elegance of the building is typical of Future Systems. Jan Kaplický (1937-2009) and Amanda Levete worked in partnership from the 1990s to translate the practice's abstracted, organic shapes into built realities. In 2003, on a far larger scale, they completed their other signature project in Britain, the Selfridges building in Birmingham's Bullring shopping centre. A huge, curvaceous department store covered in thousands of aluminium discs, it has become an internationally known exemplar of 'blobitecture'. The history of Future Systems extends back to 1979, when Kaplický formed the practice with David Nixon, an expert on the architecture of space exploration. Kaplický's complex, mesmerising drawings of proposed or imagined structures (including designs for the International Space Station) are his other great legacy. David Nixon included one, Weekend Retreat for Miss B., in his list for this book.

NatWest Media Centre
NatWest
NatWest

PECKHAM LIBRARY

36 Peckham Hill Street, Peckham, London SE15
Completed in: 2000
Architects: Alsop & Störmer – Will Alsop (1947-2018)

Will Alsop's engaging public building in the South London district of Peckham was a successful attempt to refresh one of the most widely visible and highly valued forms of civic space: the local library. It became a popular landmark as soon as it was completed, and remains so in a climate of increasingly lean library funding. Delivered on a relatively small budget, it was used in record numbers by the local community in the year it opened. The approaching visitor might see it as an upended 'L' somehow turned through 90 degrees, or perhaps as a stranded bookshelf or a propped-open book. The top two floors, cantilevered over a welcoming outside space, are the main reading and study zone. They are supported by seven steel columns leaning at seemingly random (although functionally load-bearing) angles. Separate areas for study and meetings are provided, not in conventional rooms but in several plywood-clad pods. (A favourite Alsop device, as employed more spectacularly in the Neuron Pod extension (2018) at the Blizard Institute in Whitechapel). The front and sides are covered in patinated copper. At the back, facing north, is an elevation of multi-coloured glass, with views to the city, admitting natural light without excessive direct sun. Similarly, a jaunty 'beret' structure on top of the building regulates light entering from the glazed sections on the roof.

Alsop was a restlessly inventive architect and teacher who often found inspiration in painting as a starting point for designs. With a few critical and commercial hiccups along the way, he left behind a series of widely enjoyed buildings. These include the Sharp Center for Design (2004) in Toronto, a Canadian relative of Peckham Library, raised high above the ground on twelve slanting multicoloured poles, and Chips (2009). The appearance and attitude of this nine-storey development of canalside flats in New Islington, Manchester – three irregularly-stacked slabs that really do evoke their title — emerged partly from Alsop's conversations with locals. "I like people," he told Lynn Barber in a 2007 interview. "I hope it shows."

LIBRARY

TATE MODERN

37 Bankside, London SE1
Completed in: 2000 & 2016
Architects: Herzog & de Meuron

Across the Thames from St Paul's Cathedral, and carefully proportioned so as not to overwhelm it, Bankside Power Station supplied electricity to London from 1953 until its closure in 1981. Giles Gilbert Scott's stern, brick-clad structure – boiler house, turbine hall, and central, 99-metre-high chimney tower – then sat empty for many years. It remained under regular threat of demolition until 1994, when Tate announced that it would become its new gallery of modern art. The Swiss practice of Herzog & de Meuron began a long process of repurposing and extension that only finished with the completion of Switch House in 2016, and has utterly transformed the surrounding riverside neighbourhood. The journey across the Millennium Footbridge between St Paul's and Tate Modern is now one of London's most hallowed tourist routes.

Tate Modern first opened in 2000, revealing a building that had been drastically adapted, but neither civilised nor disguised — still clearly a rugged, formerly industrial place. The Boiler House became the main network of gallery spaces, housing permanent displays and temporary exhibitions over several storeys. Meanwhile, the great void of the Turbine Hall was an instant, awe-inspiring public success. The original machinery was removed, along with the entire floor at ground level, creating a gigantic space from basement to roof, the entire height of the original building. Every year, a different artist is invited to address it by creating a new installation, drawing huge numbers of curious visitors. Olafur Eliasson's *The Weather Project* (2003) featured an immense, immersive recreation of the sun. In 2010, Ai Weiwei flooded the space with millions of hand-made, life-sized porcelain sunflower seeds. The new gallery's popularity outstripped all expectations, and Herzog & de Meuron returned several years later to create Switch House (now the Blavatnik Building). Although clad in a complementary brick, its mysterious, irregularly faceted exterior is in complete contrast to the older building. It provides 11 floors of dramatic new space, and spectacular London views from the observation deck at the top, which has proved problematic for residents of the neighbouring glass-fronted towers. The basement galleries are formed from the power station's massive concrete tanks, drained of their reserves of oil.

TATE MODERN

LABAN DANCE CENTRE

38 Creekside, Deptford, London SE8
Completed in: 2003
Architects: Herzog & de Meuron

Laban Dance Centre's history extends back to the 1950s, when Rudolf Laban founded his first school of movement and dance in Manchester. The Centre has been in London since 1975, growing into an internationally recognised school for contemporary dance. It merged with Trinity College of Music in 2005 to become Trinity Laban Conservatoire of Music and Dance, with bases in nearby Greenwich and New Cross as well as Deptford. Laban addressed its need to expand and update in 1997 with an architectural competition to build a new home, close to the Centre's previous neighbourhood and embedded in the local community.

Herzog & de Meuron's winning design is a thoughtfully interlinked complex of theatre, studios, café, library and stepped, hilly, landscaped lawns, employing colour as a unifying theme. The architects collaborated with the artist Michael Craig-Martin, who developed the wall drawings and vivid colour schemes of the labyrinthine corridors, and the ethereal effects of the building's curved façade. An external layer of tinted polycarbonate panels sits in front of the Centre's glass walls, allowing the silhouettes of dancers and gently varying coloured light through to the outside. The strategy of gently separating areas with transparent or translucent walls continues inside the two-storey building. The floors are linked by spiral staircases, with the upper level devoted to a series of studios gently flooded with diffused light. The contrastingly dark, wood-panelled Bonnie Bird theatre, designed as the heart of the complex, accommodates up to 300 people in a venue for visiting dance performers and undergraduate shows.

LONDON AQUATICS CENTRE

39 Queen Elizabeth Olympic Park, London E20
Completed in: 2011
Architect: Zaha Hadid (1950-2016)

The focus of the 2012 Olympic Games was the Queen Elizabeth Olympic Park in Stratford, East London. Starting in 2009, a huge clearance and building programme took place to construct the necessary venues, and to drive local regeneration during and long after the Games. In the jargon of the time, 'Olympic mode' was succeeded by 'Legacy mode'. The Aquatics Centre, at the south-east corner of the Park, was among the first projects to be started and the last to be finished. Its defining feature is the graceful, wavy roof of aluminium that rises from ground level over the three pools inside, echoing the flow patterns of water. Inside, the corresponding effect of the timber-clad ceiling is just as impressive, along with the elegant, smooth concrete forms of the walls and diving platforms.

Jacques Rogge, president of the International Olympic Committee, pronounced the Aquatics Centre a masterpiece on its completion; alongside the velodrome (now Lee Valley VeloPark) by Hopkins Architects, it is perhaps the best known and most widely admired architectural outcome of London 2012. It's also the late Zaha Hadid's key achievement in Britain; one of only a handful of projects that she completed in this country. Other public buildings include the Glasgow Museum of Transport (2011) and her extension to the Serpentine Sackler Gallery in Kensington Gardens (2013). Once the Olympics were over – in Legacy mode – the sculptural beauty of the Centre came fully into its own: the temporary seating wings were removed from both sides, and the spaces were filled with glass, allowing natural light to pour in. It opened to the community as a public swimming complex in 2014.

THE SHARD

40 **London Bridge Street, London SE1**
Completed in: 2012
Architect: Renzo Piano Building Workshop

Britain's tallest building (at the time of writing), the Shard has 72 floors and rises to 240 metres. It's one of a group of hyper-distinctive skyscrapers with disarmingly informal names that has come to define the skyline of 21st-century central London. As the structure rises and eventually tapers into nothing, like the church spires that partly inspired Renzo Piano in imagining its form, the use of the spaces varies accordingly: the lower floors are offices; on top of them are restaurants, a hotel and apartments; finally, there are public observation decks on floors 69 and 72. Piano became internationally known with Richard Rogers after the spectacular success of the Pompidou Centre, completed in Paris in 1977, when both architects were still in their thirties. The Shard remains his chief work in Britain. There is also Central St Giles (2010) a development of two tall buildings covered in brightly coloured terracotta tiles, near Centre Point in the West End.

The Shard's developer, Irvine Sellar (1934-2017), was a seasoned entrepreneur. In the 1960s he made a fortune in Swinging London with Mates, his revolutionary chain of unisex fashion boutiques. His tenacity and resources were severely tested in the years after he approached Renzo Piano in 2000, on the 12-year route to completing the project. Opposition from heritage groups and campaigners concerned about the impact on the historic London skyline led to a major planning inquiry; an international financial crisis followed soon after. Ultimately the project was fully realised, including the construction of a new passenger approach and concourse for neighbouring London Bridge station. The gigantic glazed facades of the building conceal clever technology to regulate heat and light within, including a complex system of automated blinds. From outside, as most Londoners experience the building, the expanses of glass reflect the changing weather and the presence or otherwise of the sun, varying the building's prominence against the backdrop of the city and the sky.

KETTLE'S YARD

(1970 & 2018 EXTENSIONS)

41 Castle Street, Cambridge, Cambridgeshire
Completed in: 1970 & 2018
Architects: Leslie Martin (1908-2000), David Owers & Jamie Fobert Architects

Jim Ede's unique fusion of gallery and home near the centre of Cambridge grew from the conversion of four 19th-century cottages in the mid-1950s, slowly undertaken with the architect and painter Winton Aldridge (1906-1997). Ede used the space to create a house of informal, unlabelled displays: a range of art works, antiques and found objects that reflect his friendships, passions and distractions across decades. The collection includes work from modern British and European figures such as Alfred Wallis, Christopher Wood, Barbara Hepworth, Henri Gaudier-Brzeska, Constantin Brancusi and Naum Gabo. Cambridge students were welcomed regularly and given personal tours.

The University agreed to take on the collection in 1966, allowing money to be raised for an extension to the house and an adjacent gallery space for temporary shows. In conjunction with Cambridge architect David Owers, this was a later project for the veteran British modernist, Leslie Martin, who had been lead designer of the Royal Festival Hall (1951, see p. 34) and was then the head of Cambridge University Architecture School. The project greatly extended the house, providing two floors of extra space for displays, an informal library, and music recitals, on a dramatically different scale to the 19th-century buildings to which it connects. Martin and Owers designed a series of calm, white-walled spaces, entered from the first floor of the original house, ingeniously and subtly illuminated from above with natural light. Incorporating places to sit, observe and contemplate, the extension successfully carries over Ede's ambition of a holistic art interior from the older house. After a two-year closure, Kettle's Yard reopened in 2018 with major enhancements. Expansion work by Jamie Fobert Architects has unified the original house, the 1970 extension and a fresh development of galleries, café and education facilities. The new buildings echo the muted lighting effects, brickwork, timber and rough plaster finishes familiar from before, ensuring a clear continuity with Jim Ede's founding vision.

SAINSBURY CENTRE FOR VISUAL ARTS

42 **University of East Anglia, Norfolk Road, Norwich, Norfolk**
Completed in: 1978
Architects: Foster Associates - Norman Foster

Norman Foster's first major public building provided a generous, innovative context for the display of art, and a distinct aesthetic experience in its own right. The Sainsbury Centre is the public home of the late Robert and Lisa Sainsbury's diverse art collection, ranging from antiquity to the 20th century. It features pieces by modern masters including Francis Bacon, Alberto Giacometti, Lucie Rie and Henry Moore, alongside related collections and a vibrant temporary exhibitions programme. The building sits on a sloping site, at the edge of the university campus meticulously planned by Denys Lasdun during the 1960s. It's directly linked to Lasdun's work by an elevated walkway to the Teaching Wall, and also within sight of his famous ziggurats of student rooms, Norfolk Terrace. At the same time, it's a quite separate entity looking out towards the adjacent park and woodland, the lake and the River Yare.

The sleek, hangar-like structure consists of a steel framework covered in aluminium panels and glazed sections. Everything service-related is accommodated in the space between its internal wall and its external cladding. Inside, this means airy, uninterrupted, reconfigurable space, housing mezzanine levels, galleries, study and research areas, a café and a restaurant. Natural light is admitted and regulated by a system of motorised louvre blinds. The modular, prefabricated flexibility of the Centre proved an influential landmark, setting a standard for the style referred to (although seldom by the architects directly involved) as high-tech. From outside, the construction method is vividly on display at each end: the structural lattice of tubular steel is exposed, surrounding walls that are made entirely of huge glass panels. Scope for future adaptability and growth was naturally built-in, and over the years the Centre has expanded eastward and partly below ground in The Crescent Wing. The Sainsbury Centre continues to excite and change without losing its essential clarity. The total concept of the building is evident everywhere, from the galleries and other public areas to the intimate connection with the landscape outside. It marked its 40th anniversary in 2018 with the autobiographical exhibition, *Superstructures*.

WILLIS BUILDING

43 **Friars Street, Ipswich, Suffolk**
Completed in: 1975
Architects: Foster Associates - Norman Foster

This breakthrough project for the young practice of Foster Associates brought international recognition and was showered with awards. "The combination of a quiet competence and technical daring will make any visiting architect feel humble about his own skills," commented the judging panel awarding RIBA's Eastern England prize on its completion. The brokers Willis Faber Dumas commissioned Norman Foster to provide a civilised modern office, palatable enough to attract employees from London to Ipswich, as well as a contemporary, energy-efficient structure. Forty years later, despite decades of familiarity, the building remains a fascinating and futuristic landmark in a Suffolk town with an ancient history as a port and trading centre.

The three main floors are completely sheathed in a curtain of dark-tinted glass: 890 panels connected at the corners and hung from the top. In daylight it appears virtually black from outside, literally reflecting its older surroundings. After dark, with internal lighting visible, it changes character to glow gently. Deep-plan and low-rise, the building expertly fills the irregular plot dictated by Ipswich's medieval street patterns – "flowing to the edges of its site like a pancake in a pan," in the practice's own description. Inside, the architects made a revolutionary open-plan workplace full of features seldom encountered in British office life at the time: a central duo of escalators to every floor in a light-filled atrium, a turfed and planted (and thermally efficient) roof garden, a staff restaurant and an indoor swimming pool. A vibrant colour scheme of greens and yellows was used for flooring and partitions. The project takes inspiration from Owen Williams's dark, vitrolite-faced Daily Express buildings of the 1930s (see p. 16) but also looks forwards, pushing ahead the accepted conventions of construction technology and office environment – although the pool, sadly, is boarded over. Testifying to its functionality and flexibility, the Willis Building remains in full use, much as it was originally configured.

A HOUSE FOR ESSEX

44 Black Boy Lane, Wrabness, Essex
Completed in: 2015
Architects: FAT Architecture & Grayson Perry

A House for Essex celebrates the complicated, ultimately tragic life of Julie Cope, from her birth on Canvey Island, via Basildon, to the moment her existence was cut short by a tragic collision with a moped in central Colchester. In the building her story unfolds in tapestries, ceramic work, woodcuts and other interior details. Fortunately Julie is a product of Turner Prize-winning artist Grayson Perry's imagination. He proposes her as a sort of exemplar of Essex women, standing for "single mums in Dagenham, hairdressers in Colchester, and the landscape and history of Essex". Her finely detailed biography is the basis for this collaboration with Charles Holland of FAT. (FAT – Fashion Architecture Taste – was the erudite, magpie-like, provocative partnership of Sean Griffiths, Charles Holland and Sam Jacob. It disbanded in 2013. You can find Charles Holland's list of favourite buildings at the back of the book.)

This astonishing building-artwork sits in isolation on the banks of the River Stour in rural Essex, as one of a network of immersive holiday homes commissioned by the Living Architecture organisation. Others have been created around the country by architects including Michael and Patty Hopkins, John Pawson and Peter Zumthor, but A House for Essex is by far the most baroque and outrageous commission to date. The outside is covered in bespoke tiles depicting symbolic details of Julie Cope's life, from safety pins to cassette tapes to the Essex coat of arms. Her pregnant figure and other sculpted symbols adorn four increasingly tall gold-coloured pitched roofs, reflecting an interior that culminates in a double-height living area. Here, the history of Julie Cope is presented in detail, including the moped that killed her off, which is suspended from the ceiling. The whimsical, emotional journey through the house takes global and local inspiration from follies, mausoleums, remote wayside chapels and fairy tale gingerbread houses, to name but a few.

HASTINGS CONTEMPORARY

(JERWOOD GALLERY)

45 **Rock-A-Nore Road, Hastings, East Sussex**
Completed in: 2012
Architects: HAT Projects - Hana Loftus & Tom Grieve

The Jerwood Gallery opened in 2012 on what had been the site of a seafront coach park, at the foot of Hastings Old Town. The location and the concept were sensitive. It was to be adjacent to the Stade: the shingle beach that is home to the town's historic fishing fleet and the venerable, uniquely Hastings phenomenon of the net shops — tall, tar-covered weatherboard huts built to store fishing nets and tackle. Other aspects of Hastings heritage include a long history of traditional British seaside tourism, considerable poverty and unemployment, and a proud, home-grown strain of bohemianism. The new gallery, initially co-funded by the Jerwood Foundation and the local council, had many different audiences to convince and became the focus of fears about gentrification of the old town. In fact, the result was a distinctive but unshowy presence. It has built a fine track record of contemporary British art shows and found its niche in the local community. The building is clad in hard, reflective black tiles whose appearance varies with the weather and the light. The surfaces complement the dark boards of the nearby net shops and also refer to the Sussex and Kent tradition of 'mathematical tiles' used to mimic brickwork on timber-framed buildings. The glaze process was developed by local company, Robus Ceramics. Inside are two levels of serene, contemplative spaces with natural light from overhead, and a café that looks out on the fishermen's beach.

Unlike many seaside culture venues, from Bexhill's De La Warr Pavilion (see p. 102) to Turner Contemporary in Margate, it has not set out to be a landmark. It slots modestly into the seaside landscape alongside older structures designed for other sorts of work and play. Its future looks bright under the new banner of Hastings Contemporary (since 2019), and with Britain's best-loved illustrator Quentin Blake as patron. While in Hastings, it would be a shame not to visit the new pier too (dRMM Architects, 2016). It won the Stirling Prize and Pier of the Year in 2017, although the ownership and approach have changed a bit since then. If you stand on it and look west, you can also see Marine Court (see p. 100).

JERWOOD
GALLERY

MARINE COURT

46 Marina, St Leonards-on-Sea, East Sussex
Completed in: 1938
Architects: Kenneth Dalgleish (1887-1964) & Roger K. Pullen

This 1930s development of flats and shops has had more than its fair share of difficulties; nevertheless, it remains a powerful presence on the Sussex seafront. It's a more overtly playful, art deco creation than Brighton's sleekly modernist Embassy Court (see p. 104), but it shares with it the quality of overwhelming its much older neighbours. Marine Court is a tall, narrow steel-framed building of 14 storeys high, grafted on to the end of a colonnaded Regency terrace. It was promoted as an advanced luxury development; services and facilities included all-electric appliances, cleaning staff, a 13th-floor sun deck, and meals delivered to residents from the building's (sadly lost) two-storey restaurant. Almost all flats have sea views and balconies. It's common to liken elegant 1930s blocks to advancing cruise liners, but few others fit the bill as enthusiastically as Marine Court: the eastern corner was modelled on the prow of a grand ship, and the upper levels are set back with a series of undulating balconies inspired by the deck shapes of Cunard's Queen Mary (the celebrated ocean liner of 1934). The conceit continued at ground level, where a long canopy with a stylised wave pattern was positioned over the dark-tiled walls of the shops, suggesting the sea, with the 'hull' of the 'ship' beneath.

Marine Court's arrival naturally made waves. A 1937 contest to name it drew several unhelpful suggestions including 'Monstrositic Mansions', 'Fallacy Chambers' and 'Mammon Court'. However, the *Hastings and St Leonards Observer* reported, "the number of sarcastic entries was very small". As the building was completed not long before the outbreak of the Second World War, it was soon commandeered for use by military personnel. In later years, as British seaside resorts suffered a general decline in prestige and visitor numbers, Marine Court entered a familiar phase of deterioration involving maintenance problems and a chronic shortage of funds. Residents included unconventional and bohemian characters attracted by its chequered history, including the writer Iain Sinclair, who characterised it in 2010 as "the ship of fools where lost souls are always welcome". In the same year, a group of flat owners managed to buy the building's freehold and began a programme of gradual refurbishment that continues today.

DE LA WARR PAVILION

47 **Marina, Bexhill-on-Sea, East Sussex**
Completed in: 1935
Architects: Erich Mendelsohn (1887-1953) & Serge Chermayeff (1900-1996)

The De La Warr Pavilion (Warr pronounced 'ware' by those in the know) emerged from an architectural competition set in 1933 by Herbrand Sackville. The 9th Earl De La Warr and Labour peer was the mayor of Bexhill, and keen to renew his unassuming Sussex seaside town with a distinctly contemporary public amenity for all. The result was one of Britain's very first, finest and fully realised public buildings in the sleek, international modernist style of the era. The clear winner from 230 entries was the design of Mendelsohn and Chermayeff, who practised together for a few years following Mendelsohn's arrival in England from Nazi Germany in 1933. Chermayeff had recently worked on the original studios at Broadcasting House in London. Mendelsohn had a distinguished track record of large-scale public buildings, working with Modern Movement luminaries including Walter Gropius and Ludwig Mies van der Rohe. Both had left for America by the early 1940s.

Their Pavilion was a startling intervention in the Victorian and Edwardian context of Bexhill seafront. Its advanced, welded-steel frame went up in a matter of days, and the whole structure was completed in less than a year. It opened to the public in December 1936 as a white-walled, terrazzo-floored temple, dedicated to conferring the health-giving properties of sunlight, fresh air and sea views on the visiting public. There were fixtures in stainless steel and chrome, chairs designed by Alvar Aalto, a theatre, a restaurant, bars, full-length balconies, a reading room and a roof terrace. On the seafront side, the focal point is the spectacular chrome-railed spiral staircase connecting all three levels, with a pendant central light fitting running through its core from ceiling to ground. After uncertain times in recent decades, including the threat of a sale into private hands, the Pavilion was reborn under the control of a charitable trust. It reopened in 2005 after careful renovation by John McAslan and Partners and now thrives as a cultural, community and entertainment venue, remaining open to all. Today, the restored building makes frequent cameo appearances on film and television when authentic, streamlined 1930s flavour is called for. For a good look at its key features in their original state, watch murder mystery *Double Confession* (1950).

EMBASSY COURT

48 Kings Road, Brighton, East Sussex
Completed in: 1935
Architect: Wells Coates (1895-1958)

Embassy Court, completed in the year after its Hampstead sibling, The Isokon, was a much bigger and more luxurious commercial project for the adventurous Canadian modernist Wells Coates. While The Isokon was conceived to provide stylishly functional 'minimum flats' for a community of young professionals, Embassy Court was always intended as plush utopianism by the seaside. There were still prominent communal facilities: a sun deck at the top, a spacious entrance lobby and lounge (with a Brighton-themed mural by Edward McKnight Kauffer), and even a residents' banking hall. But the emphasis here was on deluxe comfort and contemporary style: every flat had a balcony and many were designed with special glass 'sun parlours' connecting to the major rooms. The uppermost two floors, stepped back from the rest, featured what the publicity claimed as a unique innovation: "the first English equivalent of the Penthouse flats so deservedly popular in New York". Modern technology and flair abounded in the interiors. These included compact fitted kitchen units, tubular steel furniture made by PEL (Practical Equipment Ltd) and all-electric power with constant hot water.

The L-shaped, reinforced concrete block of 11 floors, with its uninterrupted horizontal bands of concrete and glass curving right round a seafront corner, is an unapologetic contrast to the 1820s terraces of the Brunswick Town development next door. Unlike its many detractors, Sir Herbert Carden of the Brighton Corporation saw the building as a template for the future of the town, writing in 1935: "Embassy Court, that modern block of flats designed by that talented young architect, Mr. Wells Coates, has shown us the way to build for the new age." From the 1980s, beset by complicated management problems, Embassy Court fell into serious decline, routinely dismissed as a dangerous eyesore. There followed years of passionate and expensive struggle by a coalition of flat-owners and admirers of the building's enduring spirit. 2006 saw the completion of a refurbishment programme by Conran and Partners, led by Paul Zara (whose list of favourite buildings is in the section at the end of this book). Today, its cream-coloured exterior pristinely restored, Embassy Court's emphatically modernist presence on Brighton seafront is more widely admired than at any point in its history.

TRICORN CENTRE

49 **Charlotte Street, Portsmouth, Hampshire**
Completed in: 1966 (Demolished in: 2004)
Architects: Owen Luder Partnership – Rodney Gordon (1933-2008)

Well into its second decade of non-existence, the Tricorn Centre has a passionate fan base that puts most living buildings to shame. In 38 years, it made such a dent on the consciousness of Portsmouth that it is still spawning fanzines and tribute websites. Its mythic place in local history was formally marked in 2014 by an exhibition at the City Museum called *Tricorn – Controversy in Concrete*. Portsmouth's own bespoke brutalist megastructure offered a wide variety of intriguing, sculptural, bare concrete forms on one compact site. In the best utopian practice of the time, vehicles were isolated from pedestrian users, parking at the top via huge, bold, spiral ramps. The swept-up edges of the car park levels prefigure similar concrete forms at Preston Bus Station (1969, see p. 138). Below was a wholesale market, flats, a pub, a nightclub and shops. The various entrances and passageways were optimistically intended to suggest the spirit and vibrancy of the kasbah: the neutral backdrop of the concrete shell would be brought to life by the shops and businesses inside. However, after initial success and enthusiastic praise from architectural critics, things did not develop as intended: the Centre was never properly integrated into Portsmouth's main shopping routes, and the spaces proved hard to let to high-profile stores. Structural problems with the flats meant that they were never fully occupied, and poor maintenance led to an all too predictable decline.

The Tricorn Centre presented its brutalist assets so potently that it completely polarised opinion. In 2001 it topped a BBC poll of Britain's worst buildings, even amid growing local affection and constructive ideas for its re-use. The city council authorised its premature demolition in 2004. A spokesman summarised their opinion: "The council's view is that the Tricorn has wasted the potential for the city centre for a long time." Despite several plans and promises, the site has never been redeveloped and the empty space has been a surface car park ever since. It's almost as if nothing is quite powerful enough to replace it.

CREEK VEAN HOUSE

50 **Feock, near Truro, Cornwall**
Completed in: 1966
Architects: Team 4

Founded in 1963, Team 4 comprised four young architects, two married couples, in democratically-named partnership: Su Brumwell, Richard Rogers, Wendy Cheeseman and Norman Foster. The other founding member of the practice was Georgie Wolton, designer of Cliff Road Studios (1968) in Camden, north-west London. One of Team 4's earliest commissions was Creek Vean, a private home built over three years for Su Brumwell's parents, on a steep hill overlooking the Fal Estuary at Pill Creek in Cornwall. It consists of two separate sections at varying levels, built at an angle to each other so that one overlooks the creek to west and the other the sea to the south. Both parts are subtly connected by a wide corridor with an angled, glazed roof, linking the various living areas, which was designed to display the original owners' art collection. In between, steps sweep down to the lawn, with a boathouse and the water below. The house is integrated ingeniously into its steeply sloping location, with loosely maintained planting on the flat roofs and steps enhancing the impression that it's gradually blending with its surroundings. When seen from the road, Creek Vean presents itself as two blank concrete walls, in contrast to the fabulous views available from the other side.

Team 4 would dissolve the following year as Norman Foster and Richard Rogers parted to forge their own hugely influential careers. In subsequent years, seperately exploring new approaches and technologies, they pioneered the use of more flexible and lightweight materials than the concrete blocks and slate floors that are central to Creek Vean. The practice's brief history closed with its final project, the Reliance Controls Factory (1967, now demolished) in Swindon, Wiltshire. This uncompromisingly simple industrial building was built quickly (in ten months) and economically from prefabricated metal parts. It aimed to desegregate management and employees in a series of flexible, shared spaces.

CASTLE DROGO

51 **Drewsteignton, near Exeter, Devon**
Completed in: 1930
Architect: Edwin Lutyens (1869-1944)

Edwin Lutyens is known as an ingenious, influential and prolific architect of Arts and Crafts country houses, public buildings and war memorials, including the Cenotaph in Whitehall. He was also the designer of the last castle built in England. The project was the vision of retail millionaire Julius Drewe, founder of a chain of grocery shops called the Home and Colonial Stores. Convinced of his noble Norman ancestry in the area, Drewe commissioned Lutyens in 1910 to build an immense family seat in a commanding position on the edge of Dartmoor, looking down on the Teign Gorge. Construction began the following year but was then interrupted by the First World War. With the scarcity of labour and materials, work on Castle Drogo went on for many years, and the version completed in 1930 was far smaller than Lutyens's original conception.

Despite serving no military or defensive function, Castle Drogo deftly meets the romantic expectations of the Norman and Tudor castle, with its gatehouse, portcullis, battlements, and walls of rough local granite up to 6 feet thick. There is an expertly created, fictitious impression of origins that stretch back centuries, and the character of the interiors, borrowing from the Tudor period onwards, confirms the feel of gradual, organic development. At the same time, the austerity of the outside hints at modernist simplicity, and Lutyens merged the authentic historical mood with the full range of up-to-date conveniences: lifts, modern kitchens and lighting, and electricity powered by water turbines. Castle Drogo's position puts it at the mercy of the ferocious Dartmoor weather: as early as the 1930s, serious water penetration problems were found on the expanses of flat roof, threatening the whole structure. There has been a major repair programme by the National Trust, who were given the property by the Drewe family in 1974. The castle and its formal gardens, planned by Lutyens with George Dillistone (rather than his usual collaborator Gertrude Jekyll) are open to the public.

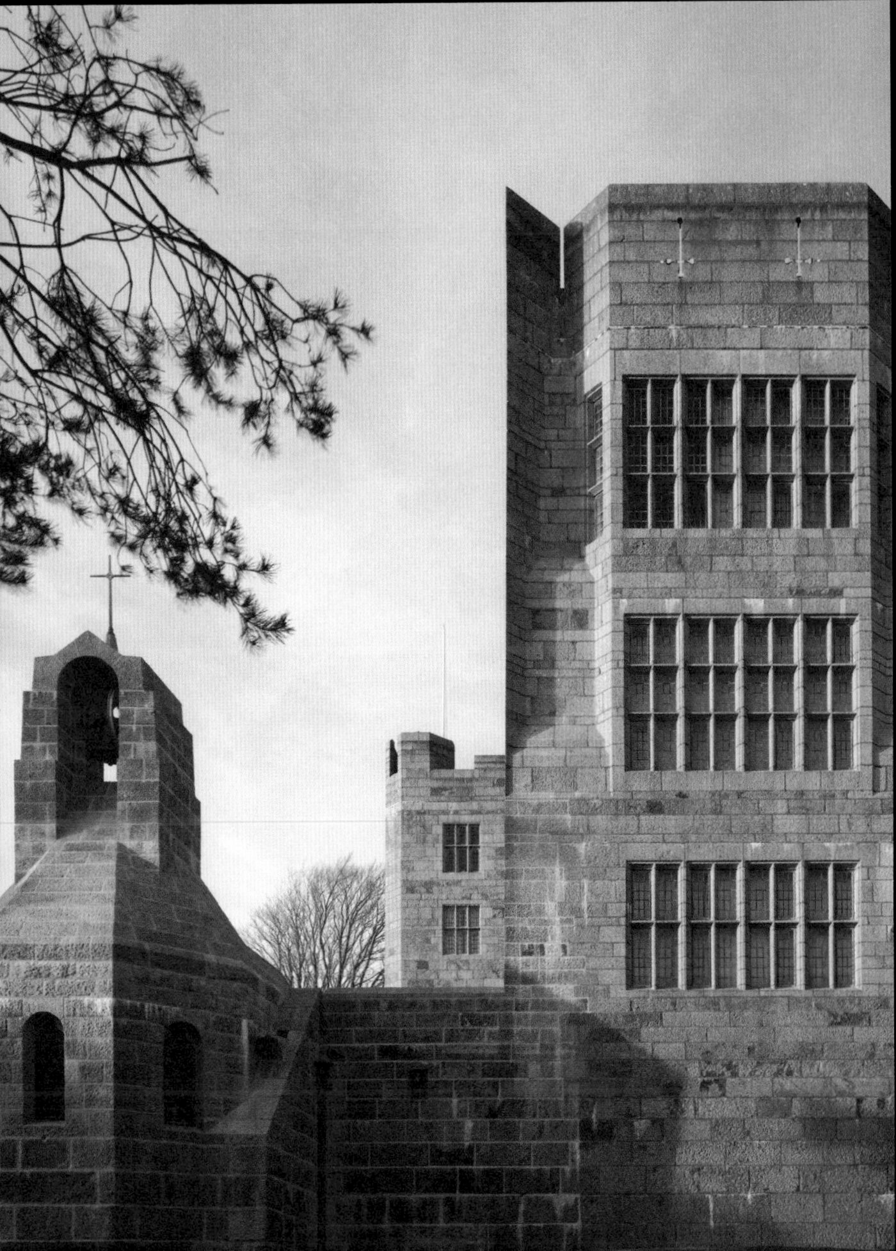

UPPER LAWN PAVILION

(SOLAR PAVILION)

52 **Fonthill Estate, Tisbury, Wiltshire**
Completed in: 1962
Alison Smithson (1928-1993) & Peter Smithson (1923-2003)

This modest weekend retreat in the Wiltshire countryside was the only house that Alison and Peter Smithson built for their own use. It was created around the remains of a demolished 18th-century cottage within a private garden. Two of the old structure's walls were kept: the garden wall against which it was built, and an end wall including the chimney. The latter became the centre of the new residence, with plywood-clad rooms created on either side. The result was a simple, rectangular, two-storey holiday home with three sides facing into the garden, and the last looking north over the countryside towards the fantastical Gothic remains of Fonthill Abbey. The upper floor is a timber frame clad in zinc. Everything at ground level can be opened up completely to the garden, simply by pushing back the glazed sliding doors. Interior and exterior spaces, as well as old and new structural parts, blend and overlap. What is an outdoor terrace for the Smithsons' house originally formed part of the indoor space in the old cottage.

The famous Smithson projects such as Hunstanton School (1954) and Robin Hood Gardens (1972, recently demolished) allowed them to realise their ideas on a far greater scale. But the small scope and deep simplicity of Upper Lawn Pavilion clearly illustrate a key interest of these two pioneering new brutalists. This relates to the 'as found' philosophy that they had first articulated in the 1950s: using contemporary materials to make an honestly modern building that embraces its surroundings. For the Smithsons, another aspect of Upper Lawn Pavilion's appeal was the stark difference between its rather spartan, crafted simplicity and the noise of modern urban life. Alison Smithson meditated on the transition between the two as they travelled regularly between London and Wiltshire in their plush Citroën DS. Her observations were published in a (now highly collectable) 1972 book, *AS in DS*. The building was very carefully renovated for new owners, with a small upgrade in creature comforts, by Sergison Bates architects in 2004.

DAVID MURRAY JOHN TOWER

53 **Brunel Centre, Swindon, Wiltshire**
Completed in: 1976
Architect: Douglas Stephen (1923-1992)

Swindon's central, inescapable landmark is a surprising, sleek tower from the future that rises to a height of 83 metres out of the shops of the Brunel Centre. It has seven floors of offices and ten floors of flats above. The Thirties-modern rounded edges, the grey-tinted windows and the aluminium panels lend it an undeniably space-age air, perhaps intended to signal David Murray John's aspirations for modern Swindon. John was Swindon's Town Clerk from 1937 to 1974, and a key figure in the Victorian railway town's post-war revival. He authorised the development of the Brunel Centre, including this tower that was ultimately named after him. The shopping complex, also designed by Douglas Stephen's practice in the early 1970s, has been altered considerably over the years, but the tower remains the same. Its admirers have found its incongruous presence inspiring in various ways. Fantastical novelist Jasper Fforde has insisted that it was extended to 91 storeys by surrealist builders working in papier-mâché. Piers Gough (who chose it for this book) describes it as "Archigram manqué". In his essay collection, *Museum without Walls*, Jonathan Meades (who chose it too) called it "the realisation of an unmade project glanced in a magazine".

Douglas Stephen founded his practice in London in 1954. It developed a strongly progressive reputation, and its personnel during the 1960s and 1970s included Kenneth Frampton and David Chipperfield. Other interesting work by Douglas Stephen & Partners includes the innovative block of maisonettes in Bayswater now called Corringham (1964) and the Rodwell Tower (1965, now 111 Piccadilly) in Manchester. The Mount (1964) in Campden Hill, Kensington is a handsome, white-rendered, Bauhaus-looking apartment block, revisiting earlier styles of modernism with similarly out-of-time tendencies to the David Murray John Tower.

MONK'S REST

54 **Hillside Road, Pinner, Middlesex**
Completed in: 1926
Architect: Blunden Shadbolt (1879-1949)

Blunden Shadbolt specialised in creating elaborately ancient-looking buildings from genuinely old recovered material, painstakingly gathered and preserved for the purpose – what we now call architectural salvage. In direct contrast to the clean lines of modernist architecture developing at the time, he constructed a series of Tudor-revival houses in Southern England from authentic, ready-aged ingredients such as moss-covered tiles and heavily-weathered timber. Monk's Rest was first built in 1924 as a display home for London's Ideal Home Exhibition in Olympia, at a time when London's suburbs were expanding and home-ownership was on the rise. The mock-Tudor style was widespread and highly popular in Britain between the Wars, but Shadbolt's unshakeable commitment to a notion of authenticity puts his work in another league. Monk's Rest incorporated wood, tile and brick retrieved from a 15th-century building (Old Friar's House) in Horley, Surrey, and its nostalgic stylings were appreciated by thousands of Ideal Home Exhibition visitors.

When the exhibition closed, the whole structure was dismantled and put up permanently in the Metro-Land suburb of Pinner, North West London. The house is half-timbered, with contrasting patterns of ancient brickwork, leaded windows, and plenty of deliberate unevenness derived from the ancient materials involved. Shadbolt perfected this approach into the 1930s, remaking and installing features like inglenook fireplaces and thatched roofs in groups of houses dotted around the South, especially in Kent, Surrey and Sussex. A related project on a grander scale is Bailiffscourt (1927) in Climping, Sussex. Now a hotel, it was built for Walter Guinness by Amyas Phillips in the style of a medieval manor house, using timber, stone, windows and many other details from the remains of ancient buildings in the area. Ernest Trobridge (1884-1942) was also building with a similar indifference to modernist approaches at this time, although he was less interested in reuse of original materials. His fascinating houses (near Monk's Rest) in Brent, North West London feature battlements, arrow slits, thatched roofs and various other eccentricities.

THE SUGDEN HOUSE

55 **Devereux Drive, Watford, Hertfordshire**
Completed in: 1956
Architect: Alison Smithson (1928-1993) & Peter Smithson (1923-2003)

This is an early commission for the Smithsons, and one of a small number of private houses that they built, following the completion of Hunstanton School (1954) in Norfolk and before the Economist Building (1964, see. p. 46) and Robin Hood Gardens (1972). The project was commissioned by Derek and Jean Sugden with the instruction to combine the characteristics of "a simple house", "an ordinary house" and "a radical house" in Watford, north-west of London. Meeting the brief, the result blended functional modernism with familiar aspects of English suburban housing, and plenty of playfulness and invention. Planned on a square, the two-floor, five-bedroom home has an exterior made of second-hand brick and a tiled roof, but pulls away from conventional uniformity with its L-shaped first floor windows and irregular placement of the other windows and doors. Inside, there are unenclosed timber stairs at the centre of an open-plan ground floor. Throughout the house different finishes (exposed concrete, brickwork, timber and vinyl floors, wood panelling) are used to denote separate areas, and there are many integral features designed by Alison Smithson especially for the house, including inset concrete shelving, kitchen units, built-in storage cupboards and a free-standing brick and tile fireplace.

Derek Sugden, a structural and acoustic engineer, met the Smithsons professionally during the 1950s. In 1963 he was a founding partner of Arup Associates, the pioneering equal partnership of architects and engineers, and went on to mastermind the concert halls at Snape Maltings, the Barbican, and Glyndebourne Opera House. The Sugdens lived the rest of their lives in the house that the Smithsons built for them. It was placed on the market, little altered since its completion, for the first time ever in 2017.

TURN END

56 Townside, Haddenham, Buckinghamshire
Completed in: 1967
Architect: Peter Aldington

Peter and Margaret Aldington built Turn End as a family home, on an overgrown plot in the historic Buckinghamshire village of Haddenham. Along with two more houses (The Turn and Middle Turn) and – crucially – the garden, they form a group that blends modernity, tradition, the indoor and the outdoor, the tranquil and the exciting. As well as applying his architectural training, Aldington immersed himself in the practicalities, from roof construction to internal joinery to plantsmanship. The house is made chiefly of concrete blocks and timber, and central to its conception is the unity of the indoor areas and the outdoor 'rooms' of the garden. The straightforward approach extends to the use of the same blocks to form internal features such as seating and storage. The house surrounds three sides of a courtyard, in a design that emphasises continuity and the free flow of space. Quarry tile floors extend uninterrupted from interior to exterior, past doors that can be folded back completely. As the building is mostly one room deep and one storey high, light penetrates from different directions throughout the day. Unexpected vistas and striking sight lines abound in a series of peaceful domestic spaces.

Pre-existing aspects of the site have been carefully absorbed into the fabric of Turn End. Long-established fruit trees remained undisturbed in the garden. A surviving wall made of wychert (the basic local building material of chalk, clay and straw, used in Haddenham for centuries) was integrated into the house. Aldington explained in an essay for the Twentieth Century Society in 2000 that his work should connect to the past, yet tell "today's story, not yesterday's negotiated with added icing sugar". The Smithsons' Upper Lawn Pavilion (see p. 112) – applying some of the same concepts to a small weekend retreat rather than a permanent family home – makes an interesting comparison. Turn End, still the Aldingtons' home, is occasionally open to the public for visits, tours and events arranged by the Turn End Trust (turnend.org.uk).

ST CATHERINE'S COLLEGE OXFORD

57 **Manor Road, Oxford, Oxfordshire**
Completed in: 1964
Architect: Arne Jacobsen (1902-1971)

St Catherine's developed in the 19th century as a university organisation catering to students too poor to enrol in colleges. Its accommodation and facilities were dispersed in various locations around Oxford. The decision to transform into a fully-fledged residential college was made in 1956, under the enterprising leadership of historian Alan Bullock (1914–2004). Once land to the east of central Oxford had been found, and funds eventually raised, the Danish architect and designer Arne Jacobsen was invited to plan a college from scratch. Jacobsen, a giant of Scandinavian modernism, was a controversial choice – Bullock told a newspaper in 1993 that he had been appointed because "it wasn't a good time for British architecture". However, St Catherine's is widely considered one of his finest achievements. He retained the time-honoured characteristics of Oxford college layout, infusing them with contemporary energy that extended to every aspect of the design.

The result is a set of concrete, glass and pale brick buildings that rework recognised forms, diluting the traditional atmosphere of cloistered privacy. The concrete-paved quadrangle has a circular lawn at its centre. Two accommodation blocks form the long sides, the glazed walls of their upper storeys extending over the ground floor to allow for covered walkways. The shorter ends of the quad are marked by the dining hall to the north and the library to the south. Planting and landscaping were an integral part of Jacobsen's project, maturing beautifully over the decades. A water garden runs along the western side of the college, with a bronze by Barbara Hepworth (*Archaean*) nearby. Jacobsen's plans were gradually completed in the years after the college's opening in 1962, and development continues, keeping faith with his original forms as student numbers expand. Jacobsen is now best known as a furniture designer, and his elegant work is much admired and imitated. The Egg chair and the Swan chair, especially, have come to symbolise mid-century modernism. The totality of his design concept for St Catherine's is felt everywhere, extending past the fabric of the building to library chairs, light fittings, clocks, and even the cutlery in the dining hall.

FLOREY BUILDING

THE QUEEN'S COLLEGE

58 St Clement's Street, Oxford, Oxfordshire
Completed in: 1971
Architect: James Stirling (1926-1992)

The third in what became known as Stirling's Red Trilogy is a horseshoe-shaped development of student accommodation in the centre of Oxford for Queen's College. It was commissioned by the Provost, Sir Howard Florey, in the wake of the critical success of Leicester Engineering Building (see p. 132) and the History Faculty at Cambridge. In common with the other projects, Stirling worked with red tile, red brick and large stretches of glazed facade. The completion of these early works of the 1960s and 70s, experimenting with space and form uniquely in their surroundings, was the basis of Stirling's reputation as both a daringly original architect and a notoriously abrasive working partner. In May 1984 (not long before he began work on No. 1 Poultry, see p. 76) the *Architectural Review* asked several British architects if there was such a thing as a British Tradition in architecture, and whether they thought themselves part of it. Most answers extended to a few hundred words, but Stirling's was more succinct: "No. Except in the worst sense of the word: English Noddyland and I am not part of it."

The Florey is raised up on a series of concrete A-frames, with an extensive, completely glazed frontage facing Stirling's versions of traditional Oxford college features, such as a cloister and a private courtyard. The student accommodation on four levels overlooks the River Cherwell and the city. Rooms on the top floor are double-height with a mezzanine sleeping area. On the other side, visible from the road, the building is almost completely clad in red tiles, with far fewer windows and the prominent concrete struts of its supporting structure on clear view; a mysterious façade, playing into the customary idea of seclusion and privacy for college residents. The finished work naturally divided opinion. Sir Howard Florey, having commissioned and championed it throughout its planning, died unexpectedly as construction began, leaving successors who were less attuned to Stirling's approach. There has also been a gap between critical esteem and flawed user experience – residents have often complained of poor sound insulation between rooms, and fluctuating temperatures. Nevertheless, this unashamedly modernist building in the heart of historic Oxford has no shortage of passionate advocates, from architects to critics to past residents.

AIROH HOUSES

AIRCRAFT INDUSTRIES RESEARCH ORGANISATION ON HOUSING

59 **Example at St Fagans National Museum of History, Cardiff**
Completed between: 1946-1951

The pressing need for decent homes straight after the Second World War called for some radical approaches to design, construction and materials. Amid devastating bomb damage, the imminent return home of forces personnel, and a lack of skilled builders, the short-term solution was to mass-produce houses from prefabricated parts. These could be transported around the country by road, and quickly assembled on site. From 1946, 'prefabs' appeared all over the nation, using the efficient wartime technologies developed by aircraft makers such as Bristol and Vickers. Despite a projected lifespan of ten years, many of these homes, and the communities they enabled, endured for decades; some survive to this day.

Under the government's Temporary Housing Programme, more than 150,000 prefabs were built in this period, about a third to designs developed by AIROH (the Aircraft Industries Research Organisation on Housing). Alternatives included the Uni-Seco (assembled by prisoners of war on the Excalibur Estate in Catford, South London) and Swedish timber kit houses used in agricultural areas. The AIROH house was a fully fitted prefab bungalow, with components manufactured on the same production lines that had only recently been producing aircraft parts. It arrived on site in four spray-painted, glazed, aluminium sections, complete with kitchen and bathroom, plumbing and wiring, and could be put together by unskilled labour in a matter of hours. Although relatively few examples survive today, the ingenuity of the AIROH house left its mark. The impetus to rewrite the rules, using materials and approaches commandeered from other fields, did not go unnoticed by subsequent generations of architects. The Prefab Museum (www.prefabmuseum.uk) is an amazing resource on this subject. You can see a well-preserved AIROH B2 house, complete with original fittings, at St Fagans National Museum of History (museum.wales/stfagans/).

COVENTRY CATHEDRAL

(THE CATHEDRAL CHURCH OF ST MICHAEL, COVENTRY)

60 **Priory Street, Coventry, Warwickshire**
Completed in: 1962
Architect: Basil Spence (1907–1976)

Basil Spence won the open competition to design Coventry Cathedral in 1951, and the significance of the project dominated his early career. "I became so engrossed in it... I lived liked a monk," he confided in an early 1970s television interview. As a major industrial centre making aircraft parts and munitions, the city of Coventry was a crucial and repeated target for the German Air Force during the Second World War. The medieval Cathedral of St Michael was devastated by a huge attack in November 1940, and the rise of a 20th-century replacement was to be a potent symbol of post-war recovery for the city and the nation. Spence delivered a building full of drama, colour and emotion, clearly modern in many of its forms and abstract details, yet also full of references to traditional church architecture and interiors.

Spence immediately understood the deep resonance of the bombed-out medieval remains. His design left them untouched and located them directly adjacent to the new building's main entrance. They are separated by an immense glass screen by John Hutton, etched with 66 likenesses of angels, in which you can see the reflection of the old as you enter the new. The screen is one of a dazzling range of works that Spence commissioned from eminent British artists and makers. Graham Sutherland's tennis court-sized tapestry, *Christ in Glory in the Tetramorph*, hangs behind the altar; the huge baptistery window – 195 individual stained glass panes of abstract design, suggesting renewal through a brightly shining sun – was designed by John Piper and realised by Patrick Reyntiens; Elisabeth Frink was commissioned to make a lectern in the form of a bronze eagle; Jacob Epstein's sculpture, *St Michael and the Devil*, is fixed to the wall next to the entrance from Priory Street. Inspired by its traumatic beginnings, the Cathedral became a focus for the promotion of world peace in the post-war era, operating the International Centre for Reconciliation until 2008, and continuing similar work today.

NEW ART GALLERY WALSALL

61 **Gallery Square, Walsall, West Midlands**
Completed in: 2000
Architects: Caruso St John Architects

Walsall's art gallery opened in 2000 in a brand-new publicly funded development that brought together the Garman Ryan Collection of modern art, the council's own art collection, and a venue for temporary shows. The imposing tower in the centre of town, on a wharf of the Walsall Canal, was an important and long-planned act of regeneration for the area. Following an international competition, it was also the first big public commission for the practice of Caruso St John. The practice has gone on to mastermind the design and remodelling of public buildings and art spaces around the world, including multiple Gagosian galleries, Nottingham Contemporary (2009) and ongoing restoration and future planning at Tate Britain.

The gallery's simple, powerful exterior form and the not-quite-regular arrangements of small windows refer to brutalism, but the scale and design also link to the older industrial and civic buildings nearby. The outside is entirely clad in pale terracotta tiles that progressively decrease in size towards the top. Inside is a series of generous, varied gallery spaces and an art library, all making impressive use of bare concrete and wood panelling in Douglas fir. The rooms are spread over five floors, served by lifts with announcements recorded by eminent West Midlands rock legend and admirer of the gallery, Noddy Holder. The permanent displays of painting and sculpture include many works by Jacob Epstein, along with Lucian Freud, Matisse, Picasso and Van Gogh. A new sculpture terrace was added on the fourth floor in 2012. The public square next to the gallery forms part of the development; it also included, in collaboration with Sergison Bates architects, that rare thing: a new-build pub.

ENGINEERING BUILDING

UNIVERSITY OF LEICESTER

62 **University Road, Leicester, Leicestershire**
Completed in: 1963
Architects: James Stirling (1926-1992) & James Gowan (1923-2015)

This was the project that created a major international profile for James Stirling. It's the first of the three works that became known as the Red Trilogy, along with the Cambridge History Faculty (1968) and The Queen's College Florey building (1971). It has the unusual distinction of appearing on a postage stamp, as part of the Modern University Buildings series, which was designed by Nicholas Jenkins in 1971. Celebrating a rich era of new campus architecture, the range also featured buildings at Aberystwyth, Essex and Southhampton. Stirling's single-minded audacity and experimental spirit continue to inspire, and the Engineering Building is among the most popular choices by contributors to this book, nominated nine times.

The radical design by Stirling, Gowan and the structural engineer Frank Newby deliberately emphasises the building's functions through striking, sculptural elements, and the extraordinary glass roof of the workshops and laboratories is its defining feature. This complex plan of opaque patent glazing is angled to provide plenty of overhead natural illumination, while avoiding strong direct sunlight. The resulting rows of tilted roof lights with diamond-shaped ends are uniquely recognisable and fascinating, as well as cleverly functional. The two adjacent towers, with their own bold, geometric profiles, contain lecture theatres, offices, study and research spaces. The red brick walls and tile cladding refer to Leicester's heritage of Victorian industry. Widely admired and treasured as it is, this word-famous listed building represents a huge ongoing conservation challenge – Jonathan Meades has called Stirling's buildings "perpetual invalids". But the work is clearly worthwhile. Following earlier refurbishment programmes in the 1980s and 1990s, a project including the total replacement of the glass roof was completed in 2017, upgrading the building to meet modern health and safety standards and renewing its lifespan for a projected further 50 years.

BOOTS D10 PHARMACEUTICAL BUILDING

63 **Thane Road, Beeston, Nottinghamshire**
Completed in: 1932
Architect: Owen Williams (1890-1969)

"The Beeston Factory – that wonder of modern industrial architecture – stands as the realisation of the Founder's dream; a perfectly equipped headquarters of an Army devoted to the service of the community." (Boots advertisement, *Nottingham Journal*, 1936)

By 1927, with hundreds of branches around the country, the Boots Pure Drug Company was already Britain's dominant chemist and beauty product retailer. Its purchase of almost 200 acres in Beeston was part of a programme of expansion and innovation, consolidating operations near their historic home of Nottingham. The aim was a super-modern base that advertised progressive efficiency to employees and customers alike. The immense D10 building was the 'Wets' factory, a four-storey concrete and glass space for making liquids, lotions and creams in the most efficient and overtly state-of-the-art manner possible. Raw ingredients entered on one side and were stowed on upper levels; manufacturing and packaging happened on the ground floor; finished products were stored ready to emerge on the opposite side. The system led to revolutionary efficiencies and the light, spacious interior made the day more tolerable for factory workers. These changes enabled John Boot, in a tradition of paternalistic interest for his employees, to reduce everyone's regular hours by half a day per week in 1934 without cutting their pay.

D10 was a first in Britain in terms of construction and size. Over an area of 695,000 square feet, a series of reinforced concrete mushroom columns support concrete floor slabs to make a huge, adaptable space, walled in glass, with the structural parts prominently on view. Thousands of glass discs set into the concrete roof allow light to flow in from above. Inside, the network of galleries and bridges across four storeys has drawn comparisons with similarly large, echoing spaces from cathedrals to prisons. The building's flexibility, movable partitioning and sheer scale have proved fascinating and inspirational to later architects. Its designer, the engineer and architect Owen Williams, is a giant of British modernism, also responsible for the vitrolite-clad Daily Express buildings in Manchester and London (see p. 16).

LIVERPOOL METROPOLITAN CATHEDRAL

64 **Mount Pleasant, Liverpool, Merseyside**
Completed in: 1967
Architect: Frederick Gibberd (1908-1984)

This Cathedral is Britain's largest Catholic church, yet it's much smaller than the original conception: the approved design by Edwin Lutyens featured a dome bigger than that of St Peter's Basilica in Rome. But the Second World War, along with spiralling costs, brought Lutyens's plan to a halt with just the magnificent crypt completed. Construction of Gibberd's competition-winning design began in 1962. Its instantly familiar shape dispensed with many of the accepted features of cathedral layout, focusing instead on the imagery of the crown of thorns. Gibberd placed the altar at the core of the entire plan, illuminated by the immense lantern tower of stained glass above, and surrounded by a congregation of up to 2000. Externally the cathedral is a concrete cone supported all round by 16 huge buttresses, whose lines continue upward to the glass tower, and finally to the metal pinnacles of the crown. Although the buildings differ in many ways, it's hard to resist comparisons to Oscar Niemeyer's Cathedral of Brasília (1970), started in 1958 – also frequently likened to a crown of thorns.

As Basil Spence had done at Coventry Cathedral (1962, see p. 128), Gibberd involved eminent British artists in the project, including many of the same names: John Piper and Patrick Reyntiens made the vast, curved expanses of abstract blue, yellow and red stained glass in the central tower, and there is a crucifix by Elisabeth Frink. In the side chapels around the perimeter of the building there is more stained glass by Ceri Richards (1903-1971) and Margaret Traherne (1919-2006). The porch at the main entrance from Hope Street accommodates four different-sized bells, above two colossal entrance doors that are the unmistakable work of William Mitchell. They depict stylised winged beasts in very deep relief, and their impact took even Gibberd by surprise. Mitchell confirmed in his 2013 memoir that "the doors are not for wimps". Gibberd's long and varied career included decades of work on Harlow New Town from the 1940s onwards. He also designed the cooling towers of Didcot Power Station (1968), six monumental Oxfordshire landmarks of which the last was demolished in 2019.

PRESTON BUS STATION

65 **Tithebarn Street, Preston, Lancashire**
Completed in: 1969
Architects: Building Design Partnership (BDP)

Today the architecture firm BDP is a major international concern, but its origins are in Preston, where it was founded in 1961 by George Grenfell Baines. Preston Bus Station was designed by Keith Ingham and Charles Wilson of BDP, and is an important piece of local, as well as national, heritage. Nevertheless, before it had reached its 50th birthday, the building was almost swept away as part of a planned retail redevelopment. That project finally stalled in the austere financial climate of 2011 and the Bus Station was saved for future generations, following an impassioned campaign by a coalition of familiar forces: dedicated local supporters, the expertise of the Twentieth Century Society, and architects citing it as inspiration. Unlike several similar attempts before and since (from Portsmouth's Tricorn Centre, demolished in 2004, to Birmingham's Central Library, demolished in 2016), protestors successfully averted the demolition of a brutalist landmark. In doing so, they made a valuable contribution to the very gradual increase in public affection for post-war concrete architecture.

Externally, the building is best known for the sculptural, ribbed, upward-swooping profile of its four car park storeys, originally left as bare concrete, later painted white. At the glass-fronted ground level, where the public wait for buses, great care was taken with the generous inside space: under the coffered ceiling there is furniture and detailing in African hardwood, carefully considered signage for departure bays, a Pirelli rubber floor and ceramic wall tiling. Everything is optimistically presented as much in the manner of an airport as a bus interchange. Despite long periods when little was invested in maintenance, the classy, robust materials have endured, and the building has been extensively renovated by John Puttick Associates. Decluttered and simplified, the Bus Station continues to serve its original purpose, having reduced the number of departure points and pedestrianised one side of the building to provide outdoor space that connects to the rest of the city.

A A

THE LAWNS

STUDENT HALLS OF RESIDENCE, UNIVERSITY OF HULL

66 **Harland Way, Cottingham, East Yorkshire**
Completed in: 1967
Architects: Gillespie, Kidd & Coia

Religious buildings were Gillespie, Kidd & Coia's main output for several decades from the 1930s onwards, but as commissions from the Catholic Church began to wane, the Glasgow practice was in demand elsewhere. As well as this work for the University of Hull, there were institutional projects such as the library at Wadham College, Oxford (1976), Cumbernauld Technical College (1978) and Robinson College, Cambridge (1980). At a time of rapid university growth, Hull appointed Leslie Martin, architect of the Royal Festival Hall, to plan its expansion. As a result, the university boasts notable modern buildings by Martin himself (Middleton Hall, 1967) and Peter Womersley (the Sports Centre, 1965). Gillespie, Kidd & Coia's contribution was The Lawns, an accommodation complex designed by Andy Macmillan (1928-2014) and Isi Metzstein (1920-2012).

It was a successful attempt to create a student community in the semi-rustic location of its own grounds, a few miles from central Hull and the main campus. Without the devotional overtones, it's an interesting comparison to the same practice's residential St Peter's Seminary (see p. 156). Along with a social centre, there are six 'halls' of tightly connected three-storey blocks, carefully ranged around the perimeter of the development. Windows and balconies are placed at a striking angle to the powerful, uniform, red brick exteriors. Neighbouring rooms are set back from each other in rhythmic, jagged progressions. Metzstein compared the interconnections and layout of the rooms, blocks and halls to cellular growth in natural organisms. The tranquil setting, and the clever balance of sociability and privacy built into the design, made The Lawns a popular student choice for many years. However, occupation has been gradually scaled down in recent times. New residents are no longer being accepted, as the university develops housing elsewhere, quoting a preference for "premium, high-quality, on-campus accommodation". The future of The Lawns is undecided, but its Grade II* listing will hopefully protect it from the sorry fate of several other post-war buildings by the same architects.

APOLLO PAVILION

67 Oakerside Drive, Peterlee, County Durham
Completed in: 1969
Architect: Victor Pasmore (1908-1998)

Although best known as an abstract artist, Victor Pasmore was also deeply interested in architecture and the interaction of art works with the community. His public art commissions included abstract murals for the Kingston bus garage staff canteen in South West London, the Festival of Britain, the University of Manchester and Newcastle Civic Centre. He became consultant architectural designer for Peterlee New Town in 1954, in the heyday of such post-war planning and construction, while teaching Fine Art at King's College in Newcastle. The Apollo Pavilion, a startling hybrid of public art work and brutalist bridge, was Pasmore's thought-provoking gift to Peterlee. It was named for the optimistic, forward-looking spirit embodied in 1969's Apollo moon landing, and made on site from reinforced concrete, straddling an artificial lake on the Sunny Blunts estate. The abstract series of rectangular forms functioned as a bridge and also, said Pasmore, as "architecture and sculpture of purely abstract form through which to walk, in which to linger and on which to play".

Always a dramatic statement in the context of the parkland and housing around it, the Pavilion's merits were in dispute as soon as it was finished. By the late 1970s it was suffering familiar problems: local government changes starved it of funds for maintenance, and it fell victim to neglect, decay and vandalism. The entrance stairways were removed to keep people off; the upper level was given over to planting. Pasmore was happy to fight the Pavilion's corner with its detractors, and remained engaged with the opinions of locals, yet the 1980s and 90s saw a concerted campaign to have it pulled down. Happily, events stalled long enough for the tide to turn. Positive pressure from Peterlee residents and enthusiasts brought about a re-evaluation, a painstaking restoration led by Burns Architects, and Grade II* listing in 2011. The Apollo Pavilion celebrated its 50th birthday in 2019, and remains a monument to the period's optimism and faith in the value of public housing and municipal planning.

DUNELM HOUSE

68 New Elvet, Durham, County Durham
Completed in: 1966
Architects: Architects Co-Partnership – Richard Raines (1929-2016)

The purpose-built centre for Durham University's student union is a bold, brutalist, five-level structure of overlapping concrete boxes, carefully designed to respond to its context on the steep bank of the Wear. Its levels step down to the river's edge, looking towards the towers of Durham cathedral on the opposite side. Descending from street level, the main route through the building is a stairway envisaged by the architects as an indoor street, linking all stages of the building and offering views on the way down. Dunelm House was made by Architects Co-Partnership, with Richard Raines leading the design of the project. The practice was founded in 1939 on egalitarian and socially progressive principles, by Kenneth Capon (1915-1988), Anthony Cox (1915-1993), and Michael Powers (1915-1994). They worked extensively in the university sector. Projects included student accommodation such as The Beehives (1960) at St John's College, Oxford, the ziggurat-style Wolfson Building (1969) for Trinity College, Cambridge, and the brutalist campus of the new Essex University from the mid-1960s.

The building relates intimately to the slightly older, Grade I listed Kingsgate Bridge (1963), to which it's almost joined. This was the last structure personally designed by the great engineer Ove Arup (1895-1988). The slender concrete footbridge – a thrill to cross – spans the gorge of the River Wear, supported on two graceful Y-shaped legs, one planted on each bank. The Arup organisation also advised on the construction of Dunelm House, and a little bust of the man himself is fixed to an external wall of the building near where the crossing starts. Sadly, the future of Dunelm House has been in jeopardy for several years. Over the decades, student numbers have grown hugely at Durham and there is an acknowledged need for new, bigger facilities. Demolition has been suggested as part of a redevelopment programme and the university has been reluctant to support listing the building while a decision is pending. Meanwhile, the exterior remains in dire need of a clean and the building awaits important repairs to its concrete fabric. Hopefully, the impassioned campaigning of architects and enthusiasts, along with a gradual increase in public affection for concrete, will generate a suitable new use for this beautifully situated and realised building.

BYKER ESTATE

69 **Byker, Newcastle upon Tyne, Tyne and Wear**
Completed in: 1982
Architect: Arkitektkontor - Ralph Erskine (1914-2005)

Newcastle City Council began pulling down the old Byker in the mid-1960s, with a promise not to disperse the established working-class community, but to rehouse residents in modern facilities on the same land in central Newcastle. Day-to-day life in the neglected network of Victorian terraces was captured by Finnish photographer and Byker resident Sirkka-Liisa Konttinen. The architect of the enormous commission to create a replacement estate was Ralph Erskine, a staunch egalitarian who had assisted in the planning of Welwyn Garden City in the early 1930s, and left Britain to live and work in the socially progressive environment of Sweden in 1939. Erskine tried hard to take residents' opinions into account when working on the project: he took a disused shop in Byker as an office, and encouraged locals to have their say as the delicate process of demolition, redevelopment and relocation unfolded in phases.

The plan incorporated a wide variety of flats and houses, with shared public space and greenery throughout, and bright colours used in the construction of doors, roofs, walkways and balconies. The estate's defining feature is Byker Wall, the winding line of flats at its northern border that varies from three to twelve storeys, built as a bulwark against harsh wind and traffic noise. Its contrasting patterns and shades of brickwork, dotted with small windows, face out defensively. On its other side, 200 acres of houses, maisonettes and towers extend south toward the River Tyne. Key earlier buildings were kept and incorporated into the new layout. The attempt to keep the original community in place was only a partial success, and the resulting estate, built across more than a decade from 1969, has never been free of the usual strife around public sector funding and maintenance. However, it remains an international landmark in large-scale, people-centred, social housing. Since 2012 the estate has been owned and managed by Byker Community Trust, who continue to refurbish and upgrade Byker in keeping with Ralph Erskine's design concepts, and in consultation with residents.

BERNAT KLEIN STUDIO

70 High Sunderland, Galashiels, Selkirk
Completed in: 1972
Architect: Peter Womersley (1923-1993)

Bernat Klein (1922-2014) was a textile designer for couture houses and an abstract painter whose talents renewed interest in Scottish wools around the world. Born in Serbia, he eventually settled in the Scottish Borders, with its rich heritage of textile manufacturing. His patronage was crucial to the career of Peter Womersley, who designed Klein's single-storey, flat-roofed home in 1957, and added this work studio within walking distance in 1972. Womersley's exciting and adventurous work ranges from Farnley Hey (the Frank Lloyd Wright-inflected Pennine home he built for his brother in 1955) to the angular, brutalist spectator stand (1964, still in use) at Gala Fairydean Football Club in Galashiels, a few miles north of the studio itself.

In the Selkirk woodland, he made a serene concrete-and-glass workplace: two floors of open-plan, glass-walled, light-filled space, with all the services grouped around the brick core in the middle. The building sits on a wooded slope, with a footbridge to the balconied upper level, cantilevered out over the ground floor. A roof terrace above extends still further. The horizontal concrete beams running the whole length of the studio are a quiet contrast with its natural surroundings of tall, mature trees. This mellow, much-admired building is possibly Womersley's most widely recognised achievement, but its future is not assured. Klein sold it in the 1990s and it has stood empty and vulnerable for much of the time since, with plans to convert it to a family home unfulfilled. The existence of a campaigning group (preserving-womersley.net) and an increasingly passionate interest in the work of the architect, are optimistic signs that the studio will find an enlightened owner and a secure future.

SCOTTISH PARLIAMENT

71 Horse Wynd, Edinburgh
Completed in: 2004
Architect: EMBT Architects - Enric Miralles (1955-2000) & RMJM

Scotland voted overwhelmingly to have its own parliament in the 1997 referendum, having been without one since 1707. There followed an international competition to create a building of great symbolic importance as well as a functional place of work for MSPs. It was won by Catalan architect Enric Miralles, in partnership with the eminent Edinburgh-based practice, RMJM. The site is at the epicentre of historic Edinburgh: by the foot of the Royal Mile, next to the Palace of Holyroodhouse and the cliff face of Salisbury Crags. The design was sensitive to the location, yet challenging. Miralles incorporated responses to Scottish culture and history throughout the diverse group of buildings he created. The work was explicitly made to belong to the locality and be publicly accessible, rather than seeming a pompous new imposition. He explained: "The building should originate from the sloping base of Arthur's Seat and arrive into the city almost out of the rock."

The evidence of craftsmanship, restless inventiveness and quality materials — granite, oak, sycamore — is everywhere. Saltire motifs are impressed into the concrete ceilings of the low-lit, almost subterranean public entrance halls. Lobby rooflights are derived from the shapes of upturned fishing boats. The exterior of the Canongate Wall is full of competing abstract shapes. At ground level, concrete panels are embedded with pieces of locally-occurring rock and carved texts. The heart of the whole complex is the debating chamber, with its immense, intricate, oak-beamed roof. Unlike the combative arrangements at Westminster, members sit in a less adversarial horseshoe formation. Throughout construction and for years after, the parliament's public image was clouded by the difficulties of its early history, as costs rose and completion time slipped. Tragically, Enric Miralles and Donald Dewar (Scotland's first First Minister, and the passionate driving force of the project) both died unexpectedly in 2000, long before work was finished. However, the completed building deeply impressed critics, and won the RIBA Stirling Prize in 2005. With levels of abstraction and variation some have found difficult, the route to public popularity has been slower, but steady.

ITALIAN CHAPEL

(ORKNEY POW CHAPEL)

72 **Lamb Holm, Orkney**
Completed in: 1945
Architects: Prisoners of War

In 1942, over a thousand Italian prisoners of war were brought from North Africa to Orkney, north of the Scottish mainland, to help construct the Churchill Barriers. This series of huge causeways, built from concrete blocks, served a dual purpose: they linked several Orkney islands together while also blocking the entry of enemy ships to the Royal Navy base at Scapa Flow. The arrival of the prisoners meant that Lamb Holm was host to a sizeable Catholic congregation without a place of worship. Somehow, they secured the camp commandant's permission to make one of their own, using two corrugated iron Nissen huts as a starting point for an ingenious conversion job.

The driving artistic force was painter Domenico Chiocchetti (1910-1999). With the help of some skilled fellow prisoners, he fashioned an entire chapel using the one available resource of concrete, along with whatever else could be begged, scavenged and repurposed. Chiocchetti painted an altarpiece of the Madonna and Child, glass panels depicting St Catherine and St Francis, and frescoes of cherubs and angels. His companions extended the conceit by decorating the interior to resemble brickwork, stone panels and intricate carving. An altar and font were made from concrete reinforced with scrap metal, and a rood screen from recovered wrought iron. The familiar semi-circular entrance to the Nissen hut was transformed by a custom-made concrete façade complete with Doric columns, a belfry and a relief of the head of Christ over the entrance. When the prisoners were released in 1944, Chiocchetti opted to stay and finish the work. He returned twice in the 1960s, bringing a set of Stations of the Cross from his home town of Moena in northern Italy. After the war a preservation committee was formed by the people of Orkney. It continues to maintain the chapel as it has become a symbol of peace and reconciliation, and a major Orcadian tourist attraction. This amazing feat of ingenuity, artisan skill and devotion, created from almost nothing in the harshest of circumstances, is open to visit all year round.

ST BRIDE'S ROMAN CATHOLIC CHURCH

73 **Whitemoss Avenue, East Kilbride, Glasgow**
Completed in: 1964
Architects: Gillespie, Kidd & Coia

Two years before finishing the ill-fated St Peter's Seminary (see p. 156), the practice of Gillespie, Kidd & Coia completed this imposing red brick brutalist church in East Kilbride, Scotland's first post-war New Town. They had been building Catholic churches in Scotland since the 1930s, but St Bride's belongs to a heritage of increasingly cherished later modernist examples of the practice. For these projects, the architects Andy Macmillan (1928-2014) and Isi Metzstein (1920-2012) worked under the freer creative climate permitted by the Church's modernising Second Vatican Council. Here, they designed a fortress-like, red brick mass, towering over the suburban housing nearby, perhaps recalling medieval, thick-walled Scottish castles. But despite its monolithic feel, the windowless exterior is full of delicate details. Textures and patterns are created using diagonally laid bricks, vertical on one elevation and horizontal on the next. The main doors, reached across a brick piazza, are neatly hidden from view as one great wall curves and sweeps behind another.

Inside the church, again faced with red brick, everything is top-lit. Natural light enters through the glazed roof and the arresting, copper-clad dormers that rise above it, clearly visible from outside. It then filters through the timber-slatted ceiling to illuminate the central space, playing off the brick surfaces and the deep alcoves accommodating holy statues. The effect conjures a more austere version of the light from the cupola in a baroque church, resulting in a powerful, subtly illuminated interior. St Bride's is an extraordinary contemporary church, developed along clearly modernist and experimental lines, but drawing on the deep reserves of its architects' historical references. After a welcome refurbishment in 2016, just one crucial aspect of the original project is now missing: the narrow, free-standing bell tower, which rose far above the main building to a height of over 30 metres. Following fears for its safety, it was taken down in 1983 and never reinstated.

ST PETER'S SEMINARY

74 Near Cardross, Argyll and Bute
Completed in: 1966
Architects: Gillespie, Kidd & Coia

Gillespie, Kidd & Coia worked as architects for the Roman Catholic church in Scotland from the 1930s, but it was after World War II, with the pressing need to rebuild and develop new towns, that they emerged as prolific designers of modernist Catholic churches. With Andy Macmillan (1928-2014) and Isi Metzstein (1920-2012) defining the practice's approach, the partnership of architect and client continued for three decades and produced daring brutalist buildings like St Bride's (see p. 154), East Kilbride (1963) and Sacred Heart, Cumbernauld (1964).

The Archbishop of Glasgow authorised plans for St Peter's Seminary in 1958, on land in a remote setting north of the village of Cardross on the Firth of Clyde. The self-contained campus was to accommodate a hundred priests in training, including a chapel, lecture theatre, library, refectory and study bedrooms. The complex, a thoughtful contemporary re-working of a traditional religious community, is probably Gillespie, Kidd & Coia's most widely praised work. Sadly, it is far more familiar as a melancholy ruin than a functioning building. Soon after its completion, the Church began to favour a less isolated approach to training priests, and St Peter's closed in 1980 without a clear new purpose. Shortly afterwards, exposed to neglect and vandalism, accelerated decline took hold and, despite passionate efforts, has never been reversed. The interior detail is lost but the building's powerful, looming sculptural forms remain: the main chapel at ground level, with three floors of rooms above, each stepped back in ziggurat form, the vaulted ceilings throughout, and the striking, domed side chapels. The exteriors, mostly bare concrete and brown pebble cladding, share an uncompromising modernist approach with Le Corbusier's Couvent de La Tourette (1961) near Lyon in France, but their ruggedness also acknowledges local building methods. In 2019 the Scottish government announced that, despite its status as a Category A listed building, St Peter's Seminary would be maintained in a state of what it termed "curated decay". It seems that its future as a premature ruin is assured.

ULSTER MUSEUM

(EXTENSION)

75 **Botanic Gardens, Belfast**
Completed in: 1972
Architect: Francis Pym (1924-2009)

Ulster Museum began as Belfast Municipal Museum and Art Gallery, in a building initially designed in 1913 by James Cumming Wynnes (1875-1944). It finally opened in 1929, delayed and only part-completed in the wake of the First World War and the formation of Northern Ireland and the Irish Free State. Francis Pym won the 1964 competition to design the museum's extension with an imposing brutalist plan that more than doubled the exhibition space. Despite his success, this was to be his only major completed project, and he left the profession shortly afterwards to become an Anglican priest.

Viewed from outside, it's better described as an implausible continuation than an extension. Despite the dramatic contrast, the ordered neoclassical style of the original building blends into the adjoining brutalist one with deliberate ambiguity, and no clearly indicated border. The enigmatic, protruding concrete boxes dominating the left-hand elevation seem to develop from the frontage on the right until they have completely taken over. The effect was clever and pleasing enough to convince the competition's eminent assessor, Leslie Martin, and it left Belfast with an internationally important modernist building. The most striking design feature is probably the thick upward curve of the concrete canopy, cantilevered over the original entrance. In a 2018 interview, Belfast-born contemporary artist Mark Clarke described the impact of visiting the Museum as a teenager at the height of Belfast's most troubled times in the mid-1970s. "It was the dark glamour of the interior that spoke to me and has informed my work ever since. The seamlessness of the outside was mirrored inside with its cutting-edge black ribbed floor tiles, concrete walls and decision-making dramatic spotlighting. It was theatrical, classy, modern and fun." A major refurbishment and alterations were completed in 2009 for the museum's 80th anniversary. The area beneath the concrete canopy was enclosed in glass to provide a café, and the main entrance was moved further along the front of the building. Pym's original gallery spaces have been completely remodelled to extend the educational and display facilities, but the museum's extraordinary, conflicted exterior remains.

APPENDIX

This book has been completed with help from 31 architects and experts.

They submitted lists of their 10 (sometimes fewer, sometimes more) favourite British buildings completed since 1918. Anything that featured on more than one of these lists was automatically included in the main section of the book. Author Matthew Freedman then topped up this initial selection to 75 with his pick of key buildings that featured only once.

On the following pages you find the names and details of everyone who contributed, as well as their complete lists, thus including many choices that did not make the final selection.

JOHN ALLAN - Avanti Architects - avantiarchitects.co.uk
Must-see project: renovation of The Homewood / Esher, Surrey (Patrick Gwynne & Wells Coates, 1939), 2004

Penguin Pool, London Zoo / Regent's Park, London NW1 – Berthold Lubetkin (Tecton), 1934

The Isokon Building (Lawn Road flats) / Lawn Road, Hampstead, London NW3 – Wells Coates, 1934

Highpoint I / North Hill, Highgate, London N6 – Berthold Lubetkin (Tecton), 1935

Highpoint II / North Hill, Highgate, London N6 – Berthold Lubetkin (Tecton), 1938

Finsbury Health Centre / Pine Street, London EC1 – Berthold Lubetkin (Tecton), 1938

Royal Festival Hall, Southbank Centre / Belvedere Road, Lambeth, London SE1 – Robert Matthew & Leslie Martin, 1951

Bevin Court / Cruikshank Street, London WC1 – Tecton (Skinner, Bailey & Lubetkin), 1954

Royal College of Physicians / St Andrews Place, London NW1 – Denys Lasdun, 1964

National Theatre / Upper Ground, Lambeth, London SE1 – Denys Lasdun, 1976

Museum of Scotland / Chambers Street, Edinburgh – Benson and Forsyth, 1998

STEPHEN BATES - Sergison Bates architects - sergisonbates.com
Must-see project: Ruthin Craft Centre / Park Road, Ruthin, Denbighshire, Wales, 2008

Upper Lawn Pavilion (now Solar Pavilion) / Tisbury, Wiltshire – Alison & Peter Smithson, 1962

Half Moon Theatre / Mile End Road, London E1 – Florian Beigel, 1984 (closed 1990, converted into a pub)

Lisson Gallery / Bell Street, Marylebone, London NW1 – Tony Fretton Architects, 1992

Astley Castle / Church Lane, Astley, Nuneaton, Warwickshire –Witherford Watson Mann Architects, 2012

Churchill College, Cambridge / Storey's Way, Cambridge – Sheppard Robson, 1968

KEITH BRADLEY - Feilden Clegg Bradley Studios - fcbstudios.com
Must-see project: Manchester School of Art extension / Cavendish Street, Manchester, 2013

1, 2 & 3 Willow Road / Hampstead, London NW3 – Ernő Goldfinger, 1938

Engineering Building, University of Leicester / University Road, Leicester, Leicestershire – James Stirling & James Gowan, 1963

St Peter's Seminary / near Cardross, Argyll and Bute – Gillespie, Kidd & Coia, 1966

Royal College of Physicians / St Andrews Place, London NW1 – Denys Lasdun, 1964

Economist Plaza / St James's Street, London SW1 – Alison & Peter Smithson, 1964

Creek Vean House / Feock, near Truro, Cornwall – Team 4, 1966

Fleet Road Estate (now Dunboyne Road Estate) / Dunboyne Road, Gospel Oak, London NW3 – Neave Brown, 1977

Willis Building / Friars Street, Ipswich, Suffolk – Foster Associates, 1975

New Art Gallery Walsall / Gallery Square, Walsall – Caruso St John Architects, 2000

Laban Dance Centre / Creekside, Deptford, London, SE8 – Herzog & de Meuron, 2003

PETER CLEGG - Feilden Clegg Bradley Studios - fcbstudios.com
Must-see project: Renovation of Queen Elizabeth Hall, Purcell Room, Hayward Gallery, Southbank Centre / Belvedere Road, Lambeth, London SE1 (GLC Architects Department, 1968), 2018

De La Warr Pavilion / Marina, Bexhill-on-Sea, East Sussex – Erich Mendelsohn and Serge Chermayeff, 1936

Coventry Cathedral (Cathedral Church of St Michael) / Priory Street, Coventry, Warwickshire – Basil Spence, 1962

Economist Plaza / St James's Street, London SW1 – Alison & Peter Smithson, 1964

St Catherine's College, Oxford / Manor Road, Oxford – Arne Jacobsen, 1964

Lloyd's Building / Lime Street, London EC3 – Richard Rogers Partnership, 1986

Engineering Building, University of Leicester / University Road, Leicester, Leicestershire – James Stirling and James Gowan, 1963

National Theatre / Upper Ground, Lambeth, London SE1 – Denys Lasdun, 1976

Alexandra & Ainsworth Estate / Camden, London NW8 – Neave Brown, 1978

Cripps Building, St John's College, Cambridge / Northampton Street, Cambridge – Powell & Moya, 1967

Tate Modern / Bankside, London SE1 – Herzog & de Meuron, 2000/2016

NIGEL COATES - nigelcoates.com

Must-see project: Geffrye Museum New Wing / Kingsland Road, London E2
Branson Coates Architecture, 1998

Scottish Parliament / Horse Wynd, Edinburgh – Enric Miralles, 2004

HMS Belfast / The Queen's Walk, London SE1 – Director of Naval Construction, Royal Corps of Naval Constructors, 1939

St Olaf House / Tooley Street, London SE1 – Harry Stuart Goodhart-Rendel, 1932

Coventry Cathedral (Cathedral Church of St Michael) / Priory Street, Coventry, Warwickshire – Basil Spence, 1962

Tate Modern, Switch House / Bankside, London SE1 – Herzog & de Meuron, 2016

Boots D10 Pharmaceutical Building / Thane Road, Beeston, Nottinghamshire – Owen Williams, 1932

Pimlico School / Lupus Street, Pimlico, London SW1 – John Bancroft, GLC Architecture Department, 1970 (demolished in 2010)

International Terminal Waterloo / Waterloo Road, London SE1 – Nicholas Grimshaw, 1993

Peckham Library / Peckham Hill Street, Peckham, London SE15 – Will Alsop (Alsop & Störmer), 2000

Florey Building / St Clement's Street, Oxford – James Stirling, 1971

Lord's Media Centre / Lord's Cricket Ground, St John's Wood Road, London NW8 – Future Systems, 1999

RICHARD HYWEL EVANS - Studio RHE - studiorhe.com

Must-see project: The Alphabeta Building / Finsbury Square, London, EC1, 2016

Lloyd's Building / Lime Street, London EC3 – Richard Rogers Partnership, 1986

Willis Building / Friars Street, Ipswich, Suffolk – Foster Associates, 1975

McLaren Technology Centre / Chertsey Road, Woking, Surrey – Norman Foster, 2003

Barbican Estate / London EC2 – Chamberlin, Powell and Bon 1982

Lord's Cricket Ground Mound Stand / Lord's Cricket Ground, St John's Wood Road, London NW8 – Hopkins Architects, 1987

Broadcasting House / Portland Place, London W1 – George Val Myer & F J Watson Hart, 1932

Isokon building (Lawn Road flats) / Lawn Road, Hampstead, London NW3 – Wells Coates, 1934

Daily Express Building, London / Fleet Street, London EC4 – Ellis and Clarke & Owen Williams, 1932

Alexandra & Ainsworth Estate / Camden, London NW8 – Neave Brown, 1978

KATHRYN FERRY - writer, historian, seaside expert - kathrynferry.co.uk
The Nation's Host: Butlin's and the Story of the British Seaside (2016)
Bungalows (2014)

De La Warr Pavilion / Marina, Bexhill-on-Sea, East Sussex – Erich Mendelsohn & Serge Chermayeff, 1936

San Remo Towers / Sea Road, Boscombe, Bournemouth, Dorset – Hector O'Hamilton, 1935-8

Casino, Blackpool Pleasure Beach / The Sandcastle, Promenade, Blackpool, Lancashire – Joseph Emberton, 1940

St Peter's Church, Gorleston / Lowestoft Road, Gorleston-on-Sea, Great Yarmouth, Norfolk – Eric Gill, 1939

Royal Festival Hall, Southbank Centre / Belvedere Road, Lambeth, London SE1 – Robert Matthew & Leslie Martin, 1951

Pagoda beach huts / Mablethorpe, Lincolnshire, 1950s

Deal Pier - pier head café/ Beach Street, Deal – Sir W. Halcrow & Partners / Niall McLaughlin Architects, 1957 / 2008

Isle of Man Sea Terminal / Douglas, Isle of Man – Davidson Marsh, 1965

Judge Business School, University of Cambridge / Trumpington Street, Cambridge, Cambridgeshire – John Outram, 1995

Hastings Contemporary (Jerwood Gallery) / Rock-A-Nore Road, Hastings, East Sussex – Hana Loftus & Tom Grieve, 2012

JENNY FLEMING – Cuozzo Fleming – cuozzo-fleming.com
Must-see project: The Pavilion House / Sydenham Hill, London SE26, 2019

Barbican Estate / London EC2 – Chamberlin, Powell and Bon, 1982

Golden Lane Estate / Fann Street, London EC1 – Chamberlin, Powell and Bon, 1962

Ulster Museum (extension) / Botanic Gardens, Belfast – Francis Pym, 1972

Transport House, Belfast / High Street, Belfast, Northern Ireland – J.J. Brennan, 1959

Elephant and Rhinoceros Pavilion, London Zoo / Regent's Park, London NW1 – Hugh Casson (Casson, Conder & Ptns), 1965

Penguin Pool, London Zoo / Regent's Park, London NW1 – Berthold Lubetkin (Tecton), 1934

Highpoint / North Hill, Highgate, London N6 – Berthold Lubetkin (Tecton), 1935/8

Centre Point / New Oxford Street, London WC1 – Richard Seifert & Partners - George Marsh, 1966

1 Kemble Street (Space House) / London WC2 – Richard Seifert & Partners - George Marsh, 1968

Royal College of Physicians / St Andrews Place, London NW1 – Denys Lasdun, 1964

Renovation of Queen Elizabeth Hall, Purcell Room, Hayward Gallery / Southbank Centre, Belvedere Road, Lambeth, London SE1 (GLC Architects Department, 1968) – Project architect: Richard Battye, Feilden Clegg Bradley Studios, 2018

No.1 Poultry (unbuilt design) / London – L. Mies Van der Rohe, late 1960s

NORMAN FOSTER – Foster + Partners – fosterandpartners.com
Must-see project: Sainsbury Centre for Visual Arts, University of East Anglia / Norfolk Road, Norwich, Norfolk, 1978

Peter Jones department store / Sloane Square, Chelsea, London SW1 – William Crabtree, Slater Moberly & C H Reilly, 1937

De La Warr Pavilion / Marina, Bexhill-on-Sea, East Sussex – Erich Mendelsohn & Serge Chermayeff, 1936

Daily Express Building, Manchester / George Leigh St, Ancoats, Manchester – Owen Williams, 1939

Jodrell Bank Observatory, University of Manchester / Lower Withington, Macclesfield, Cheshire – Bernard Lovell, astronomer; Charles Husband, engineer, 1957

AIROH house (e.g. at St Fagans National Museum of History, Cardiff, Wales) – Aircraft Industries Research Organisation on Housing, 1940s

St Catherine's College, Oxford / Manor Road, Oxford, Oxfordshire – Arne Jacobsen, 1964

Engineering Building, University of Leicester / University Road, Leicester, Leicestershire – James Stirling & James Gowan, 1963

Centre Point / New Oxford Street, London WC1 – Richard Seifert & Partners - George Marsh, 1966

A Walking City – Ron Herron (Archigram), 1964-66

Concorde – Aérospatiale & the British Aircraft Corporation (BAC), 1969

PIERS GOUGH - CZWG Architects - czwg.com
Must-see project: 29 Mill Street / China Wharf, London SE1, 1982-3

Cenotaph / Whitehall, London SW1 –
Edwin Lutyens, 1920

Odeon Cinema, Leicester Square / Leicester Square, London WC2 –
Harry Weedon & Andrew Mather, 1937

Barbican Estate / London EC2 –
Chamberlin, Powell and Bon, 1982

1 Kemble Street (Space House) / London WC2 –
Richard Seifert & Partners - George Marsh, 1968

David Murray John Tower / Brunel Centre, Swindon, Wiltshire –
Douglas Stephen, 1976

Lloyd's Building / Lime Street, London EC3 –
Richard Rogers Partnership, 1986

No. 1 Poultry / London EC2 –
James Stirling & Michael Wilford, 1997

Scottish Parliament / Horse Wynd, Edinburgh –
Enric Miralles, 2004

Selfridges & Co. Birmingham / The Bullring, Park Street, Birmingham – Future Systems, 2003

Laban Dance Centre / Creekside, Deptford, London SE8 –
Herzog & de Meuron, 2003

Chips, New Islington / Lampwick Lane, New Islington, Manchester –
Will Alsop (Alsop Architects), 2009

JOHN GRINDROD – writer – dirtymodernscoundrel.co.uk
Outskirts: Living Life on the Edge of the Green Belt (2017)
Concretopia: A Journey Around the Rebuilding of Postwar Britain (2013)

Coventry Cathedral (Cathedral Church of St Michael) / Priory Street, Coventry, Warwickshire – Basil Spence, 1962

National Theatre / Upper Ground, Lambeth, London SE1 – Denys Lasdun, 1976

De La Warr Pavilion / Marina, Bexhill-on-Sea, East Sussex – Erich Mendelsohn & Serge Chermayeff, 1936

Dawson's Heights / Dunstans Road, Dulwich, London SE22 – Kate Macintosh, 1972

NLA Tower / Addiscombe Road, Croydon – Richard Seifert & Partners, 1970

Bernat Klein Studio / High Sunderland, Galashiels, Selkirk – Peter Womersley, 1972

The Lawn / Harlow, Essex – Frederick Gibberd, 1951

The Sugden House / Devereux Drive, Watford, Hertfordshire – Alison & Peter Smithson, 1956

Byker Estate / Byker, Newcastle upon Tyne – Ralph Erskine (Arkitektkontor), 1982

Westminster Underground Station / Bridge Street, London SW1 – Hopkins Architects, 1999

IVAN HARBOUR – Rogers Stirk Harbour + Partners – rsh-p.com
Must-see project: Maggie's West London Centre, Charing Cross Hospital / Fulham Palace Road, London W6, 2008

Mackintosh building, Glasgow School of Art / Renfrew Street, Glasgow – Charles Rennie Mackintosh, 1909 (destroyed by fire in 2018)

Boots D10 Pharmaceutical Building / Thane Road, Beeston, Nottinghamshire – Owen Williams, 1932

AIROH house (e.g. at St Fagans National Museum of History, Cardiff, Wales) – Aircraft Industries Research Organisation on Housing, 1940s

Keeling House / Claredale Street, Bethnal Green, London E2 – Denys Lasdun, 1955

Engineering Building, University of Leicester / University Road, Leicester, Leicestershire – James Stirling & James Gowan, 1963

Economist Plaza / St James's Street, London SW1 – Alison & Peter Smithson, 1964

Royal College of Physicians / St Andrews Place, London NW1 – Denys Lasdun, 1964

Houses in Walters Way / Walters Way, Honor Oak Park, London SE23 – Walter Segal, 1984

Lloyd's Building / Lime Street, London EC3 – Richard Rogers Partnership, 1986

Stansted Airport / Bassingbourn Road, Stansted, Essex – Foster Associates, 1991

CLAIRE HARPER & JAMES PERRY – Harper Perry – harperperry.co.uk
(See also: somethingconcreteandmodern.co.uk)
Must-see project: Creativity Studio, Centre for Life / Times Square, Newcastle Upon Tyne, 2019

St Bride's Roman Catholic Church / Whitemoss Ave, East Kilbride, Glasgow – Gillespie, Kidd & Coia, 1964

Salvation Army Men's Palace / City Road, Newcastle Upon Tyne – Ryder and Yates, 1974

Highgate New Town / Highgate, London N19 – Peter Tábori, 1979

Dunelm House / New Elvet, Durham, County Durham – Architects Co-Partnership, 1966

Apollo Pavilion / Oakerside Drive, Peterlee, County Durham – Victor Pasmore, 1969

Houses at Branch Hill / Camden, London, NW3 – Benson & Forsyth, 1970

Kingsgate Bridge / Durham, County Durham – Ove Arup, 1963

Redcar Library / Coatham Road, Redcar, North Yorkshire – Ahrends, Burton & Koralek, 1971 (demolished in 2011)

Norgas House / Northumbrian Way, Killingworth, Newcastle upon Tyne – Ryder and Yates, 1965 (demolished in 2013)

Cummins Engines, Components Plant Darlington / Yarm Road, Darlington, County Durham – Roche Dinkeloo, 1966

ELAIN HARWOOD - architectural historian, Historic England - historicengland.org.uk

Art Deco Britain: Buildings of the interwar years (2019)
Space, Hope, and Brutalism: English Architecture, 1945-1975 (2015)

Finsbury Health Centre / Pine Street, London EC1 – Berthold Lubetkin (Tecton), 1938

Royal Festival Hall, Southbank Centre / Belvedere Road, Lambeth, London SE1 – Robert Matthew & Leslie Martin, 1951

Byker Estate / Byker, Newcastle upon Tyne – Ralph Erskine (Arkitektkontor), 1982

Preston Bus Station / Tithebarn Street, Preston, Lancashire – Keith Ingham & Charles Wilson (BDP), 1969

Granada Cinema, Tooting / Mitcham Road, Tooting, London SW17 – Cecil Masey, 1931

St Peter's Seminary / near Cardross, Argyll and Bute – Gillespie, Kidd & Coia, 1966

St Catherine's College, Oxford / Manor Road, Oxford, Oxfordshire – Arne Jacobsen, 1964

Engineering Building, University of Leicester / University Road, Leicester, Leicestershire – James Stirling & James Gowan, 1963

Creek Vean House / Feock, near Truro, Cornwall – Team 4, 1966

Upper Lawn Pavilion (now Solar Pavilion) / Tisbury, Wiltshire – Alison & Peter Smithson, 1962

BIRKIN HAWARD - birkinhaward.com - vhh.co.uk
Must-see project: Katharine Stephen Rare Books Library, Newnham College / Sidgwick Avenue, Cambridge – van Heyningen and Haward Architects, 1983

Quarr Abbey / Quarr Road, Ryde, Isle of Wight – Dom Paul Bellot, 1914

New Ways / Wellingborough Road, Abington, Northampton, Northamptonshire – Peter Behrens, 1926

Church of St Andrew / St Andrews Road, Felixstowe, Suffolk – Hilda Mason & Raymond Erith, 1931

85–91 Genesta Road / Plumstead, London SE18 – Berthold Lubetkin & A. V. Pilichowski, 1934

The Sugden House / Devereux Drive, Watford, Hertfordshire – Alison & Peter Smithson, 1956

The Lawns, Student Halls of Residence, University of Hull / Harland Way, Cottingham, East Yorkshire – Gillespie, Kidd & Coia, 1967

Setchell Road Estate / Setchell Road, Bermondsey, London SE1 – Neylan & Ungless, 1978

David Mellor Offices and Showroom / Shad Thames, London SE1 – Hopkins Architects, 1991

Canary Wharf Underground Station / Canary Wharf, London E14 – Foster + Partners, 1999

Old Shed New House / North Yorkshire – Tonkin Liu, 2018

SIMON HENLEY – Henley Halebrown – henleyhalebrown.com
Redefining Brutalism (2017) / *The Architecture of Parking* (2007)
Must-see project: Chadwick Hall, Roehampton University / Roehampton Lane, London SW15, 2016

Castle Drogo / Drewsteignton, near Exeter, Devon – Edwin Lutyens, 1930

Engineering Building, University of Leicester / University Road, Leicester, Leicestershire – James Stirling & James Gowan, 1963

Florey Building / St Clement's Street, Oxford – James Stirling, 1971

St Bride's Roman Catholic Church / Whitemoss Ave, East Kilbride, Glasgow – Gillespie, Kidd & Coia, 1964

St Peter's Seminary / near Cardross, Argyll and Bute – Gillespie, Kidd & Coia, 1966

Upper Lawn Pavilion (now Solar Pavilion) / Tisbury, Wiltshire – Alison & Peter Smithson, 1962

Economist Plaza / St James's Street, London SW1 – Alison & Peter Smithson, 1964

Hayward Gallery, Queen Elizabeth Hall & Purcell Room, Southbank Centre / Belvedere Road, Lambeth, London SE1 – GLC Architects Department, 1968

National Theatre / Upper Ground, Lambeth, London SE1 – Denys Lasdun, 1976

Lisson Gallery / Bell Street, Marylebone, London NW1 – Tony Fretton Architects, 1992

BEVIS HILLIER - author and journalist
Co-founder of the Thirties Society, forerunner of the 20th Century Society
Art Deco of the 20s and 30s (1968)
Decorative Arts of the Forties and Fifties: Austerity / Binge (1975)

Adelphi Theatre (1930 rebuild) / Strand, London WC2 – Ernest Schaufelberg, 1930

Strand Palace Hotel / Strand, London WC2 – Deco additions by Oliver P. Bernard, 1928 (now removed - some saved by the Victoria & Albert Museum)

Odeon Cinema Redhill / Station Road, Redhill, Surrey – Andrew Mather, 1938

De La Warr Pavilion / Marina, Bexhill-on-Sea, East Sussex – Erich Mendelsohn & Serge Chermayeff, 1936

Natural History Museum, East Wing extension / Cromwell Road, London SW7 – W. Kendall & Rolland Greatrex, E. Bedford (Ministry of Public Building and Works), 1975

Daily Express Building / Fleet Street, London EC4 – Ellis and Clarke & Owen Williams, 1932

The Shard / London Bridge Street, London SE1 – Renzo Piano Building Workshop, 2012

MI6 building / Albert Embankment, Lambeth, London SE1 – Terry Farrell, 1994

Royal Festival Hall, Southbank Centre / Belvedere Road, Lambeth, London SE1 – Robert Matthew & Leslie Martin, 1951

Hoover Building / Western Avenue, Perivale – Wallis, Gilbert and Partners, 1933

A House for Essex / Black Boy Lane, Wrabness, Essex – FAT Architecture & Grayson Perry, 2015

30 St Mary Axe (The Gherkin) / London EC3 – Foster + Partners, 2004

Eltham Palace (Deco additions) / Court Yard, London SE9 – Seely & Paget, 1935

Broadcasting House / Portland Place, London W1 – George Val Myer & F J Watson Hart, 1932

Lloyd's Building / Lime Street, London EC3 – Richard Rogers Partnership, 1986

Park Lane Hotel (Sheraton Grand London Park Lane) / Piccadilly, London W1 – Adie, Button & Partners, 1927

Chestergate House (as in 1970s) / 253 Vauxhall Bridge Road, London SW1 – Sir John Burnet, Tait & Partners, 1962

CHARLES HOLLAND – Charles Holland Architects – charleshollandarchitects.co.uk
Must-see project: A House for Essex / Black Boy Lane, Wrabness, Essex
FAT Architecture & Grayson Perry, 2015

Engineering Building, University of Leicester / University Road, Leicester, Leicestershire – James Stirling & James Gowan, 1963

Turn End / Haddenham, Buckinghamshire – Peter Aldington, 1967

Davy Place / Loddon, Norwich, Norfolk – Tayler and Green, 1963

Royal College of Physicians / St Andrews Place, London NW1 – Denys Lasdun, 1964

Wood Street Police Station / Wood Street, London EC2 – McMorran & Whitby, 1966

The Sugden House / Devereux Drive, Watford, Hertfordshire – Alison & Peter Smithson, 1956

Pumping Station, Isle of Dogs / Stewart Street, Isle of Dogs, London E14 – John Outram, 1988

Sainsbury Centre for Visual Arts, University of East Anglia / Norfolk Road, Norwich, Norfolk – Foster Associates, 1978

Lloyd's Building / Lime Street, London EC3 – Richard Rogers Partnership, 1986

Nottingham Contemporary / Weekday Cross, Nottingham, Nottinghamshire – Caruso St John, 2009

Peckham Library / Peckham Hill Street, Peckham, London SE15 – Will Alsop (Alsop & Störmer), 2000

OWEN HOPKINS - architectural writer, Senior Curator of Exhibitions and Education at Sir John Soane's Museum, London WC2 - owenhopkins.co.uk
Lost Futures: The Disappearing Architecture of Post-War Britain (2017)
Mavericks: Breaking the Mould of British Architecture (2016)

A House for Essex / Black Boy Lane, Wrabness, Essex – FAT Architects & Grayson Perry, 2015

Brandon Estate / Otto Street, Southwark, London SE17 – LCC team led by Ted Hollamby, 1903-14

Trinity Square car park / Trinity Square, Gateshead, Tyne and Wear – Rodney Gordon & Owen Luder, 1967

Pumping Station, Isle of Dogs / Stewart Street, Isle of Dogs, London E14 – John Outram, 1988

No. 1 Poultry / London EC2 – James Stirling & Michael Wilford, 1997

Castle Drogo / Drewsteignton, near Exeter, Devon – Edwin Lutyens, 1930

Snowdon Aviary, London Zoo / Regent's Park, London NW1 – Cedric Price, Frank Newby & Lord Snowdon, 1965

Arnos Grove Underground Station / Bowes Road, Arnos Grove, London N11 – Charles Holden, 1932

Balfron Tower / St Leonards Road, Poplar, London E14 – Ernő Goldfinger, 1967

DAVID JENKINS – publisher – circapress.com
Peter Salter – Walmer Yard (2019)
Archigram: The Book (2018)

Peckham Library / Peckham Hill Street, Peckham, London SE15 – Will Alsop (Alsop & Störmer), 2000

Engineering Building, University of Leicester / University Road, Leicester, Leicestershire – James Stirling & James Gowan, 1963

Sainsbury Centre for Visual Arts, University of East Anglia / Norfolk Road, Norwich, Norfolk – Foster Associates, 1978

Lord's Media Centre / Lord's Cricket Ground, St John's Wood Road, London NW8 – Future Systems, 1999

Creek Vean House / Feock, near Truro, Cornwall – Team 4, 1966

Boots D10 Pharmaceutical Building / Thane Road, Beeston, Nottinghamshire – Owen Williams, 1932

The Mount / Bedford Gardens, London W8 – Douglas Stephen, 1964

Highpoint I / North Hill, Highgate, London, N6 – Berthold Lubetkin (Tecton), 1935

Elephant and Rhinoceros Pavilion, London Zoo / Regent's Park, London NW1 – Hugh Casson (Casson, Conder & Ptns), 1965

Royal Corinthian Yacht Club / The Quay, Burnham-on-Crouch, Essex – Joseph Emberton, 1931

OWEN LUDER - Owen Luder Partnership
President of the Royal Institute of British Architects, 1981-1983 & 1995-1997
Must-see project: Hendon Hall Court, Parson Street, Hendon, London NW4, 1966

Highpoint I & II / North Hill, Highgate, London, N6 – Berthold Lubetkin (Tecton), 1935 & 1938

Royal College of Physicians / St Andrews Place, London NW1 – Denys Lasdun, 1964

De La Warr Pavilion / Marina, Bexhill-on-Sea, East Sussex – Erich Mendelsohn & Serge Chermayeff, 1936

RIBA headquarters / Portland Place, London W1 – Grey Wornum, 1934

Britannic House / Finsbury Circus, London EC2 – Edwin Lutyens, 1927

Royal Festival Hall, Southbank Centre / Belvedere Road, Lambeth, London SE1 – Robert Matthew & Leslie Martin, 1951

Willis Building / Friars Street, Ipswich, Suffolk – Foster Associates, 1975

Lloyd's Building / Lime Street, London EC3 – Richard Rogers Partnership, 1986

Tate Modern, Bankside Power station / Bankside, London SE1 – Herzog & de Meuron, 2000

Peter Jones department store / Sloane Square, Chelsea, London SW1 – William Crabtree, Slater Moberly & C H Reilly, 1939

JONATHAN MEADES – writer, journalist, essayist, film-maker – jonathanmeades.co.uk
Bunkers, Brutalism and Bloodymindedness: Concrete Poetry (BBC Four, 2014)
Museum Without Walls (2012)

David Murray John Tower / Brunel Centre, Swindon, Wiltshire – Douglas Stephen, 1976

Cliff Road Studios / Cliff Road Studios, Cliff Road, London NW1 – Georgie Wolton (Team 4), 1968

Lloyd's Building / Lime Street, London EC3 – Richard Rogers Partnership, 1986

Tricorn Centre / Charlotte Street, Portsmouth, Hampshire – Rodney Gordon & Owen Luder, 1966 (demolished in 2004)

Lecture Theatre Block, Brunel University London / Kingston Lane, Uxbridge, Middlesex – Richard Sheppard, Robson and Partners, 1966

Royal College of Art / Kensington Gore, Kensington, London SW7 – H. T. Cadbury-Brown, with Sir Hugh Casson & Robert Goodden, 1963

Our Lady Help of Christians / East Meadway, Tile Cross, Birmingham – Richard Gilbert Scott, 1967

Houses in Stag Lane, Buck Lane, etc. / Kingsbury, London NW9 – Ernest Trobridge, 1926

Hyde Park Barracks / Knightsbridge, London SW7 – Basil Spence, 1970

Monk's Rest / Hillside Road, Pinner Hill, Middlesex – Blunden Shadbolt, 1926

DAVID NIXON - space architect, industrial designer - davidnixon.eu
Co-founder Future Systems
International Space Station: Architecture Beyond Earth (2016)

AIROH house (e.g. at St Fagans National Museum of History, Cardiff, Wales) – Aircraft Industries Research Organisation on Housing, 1940s

Willis Building / Friars Street, Ipswich, Suffolk – Foster Associates, 1975

RMS Queen Mary / Clydebank, West Dunbartonshire, Scotland – John Brown & Company, 1934

Bailey bridges – Donald Bailey, 1941

Snowdon Aviary, London Zoo / Regent's Park, London NW1 – Cedric Price, Frank Newby & Lord Snowdon, 1965

Inmos Microprocessor Factory / Newport, South Wales – Richard Rogers Partnership, 1982

St George's Fields Apartments / Albion Street, London W2 – Design 5, 1973

2001: A Space Odyssey film sets, Boreham Wood / MGM-British studios, Borehamwood, Hertfordshire – Stanley Kubrick, Frederick I. Ordway III, Douglas Trumbull a.o., 1968

Royal College of Art / Kensington Gore, Kensington, London SW7 – H. T. Cadbury-Brown, with Sir Hugh Casson & Robert Goodden, 1963

Project 005 – Weekend Retreat for Miss B. – Jan Kaplický, 1980

STEFI ORAZI – writer, graphic designer – stefiorazi.co.uk
Modernist Estates Europe: The buildings and the people who live in them today (2019)
The Barbican Estate (2018)

Post Office Tower (now BT Tower) / Cleveland Street, London W1 – Eric Bedford et al., 1964

Highpoint / North Hill, Highgate, London, N6 – Berthold Lubetkin (Tecton), 1935 & 1938

Barbican Estate / London EC2 – Chamberlin, Powell and Bon, 1982

St Peter's Seminary / near Cardross, Argyll and Bute – Gillespie, Kidd & Coia, 1966

The Homewood / Portsmouth Road, Esher, Surrey – Patrick Gwynne, 1939

Isokon building (Lawn Road flats) / Lawn Road, Hampstead, London NW3 – Wells Coates, 1934

Houses at Branch Hill / Camden, London NW3 – Benson and Forsyth, 1970

Brunswick Centre / Bloomsbury, London WC1 – Patrick Hodgkinson, 1972

Apollo Pavilion / Oakerside Drive, Peterlee, County Durham – Victor Pasmore, 1969

National Theatre / Upper Ground, Lambeth, London SE1 – Denys Lasdun, 1976

ALAN POWERS – historian of architecture and design, Trustee and former Chairman of the 20th Century Society

Bauhaus Goes West: Modern Art and Design in Britain and America (2019)
100 Years of Architecture (2016)

Turn End / Haddenham, Buckinghamshire – Peter Aldington, 1967

St Paul's, Bow Common / St Paul's Way, London E3 – Robert Maguire & Keith Murray, 1960

House in Aldeburgh (the architect's home) / Church Walk, Aldeburgh, Suffolk – H. T. Cadbury-Brown, 1962

The Studio / Duke's Head Yard, Highgate, London N6 – Herbert Tayler & David Green, 1939

Abbey Church, Worth Abbey / Paddockhurst Road, Turners Hill, West Sussex – Francis Pollen, 1975

Gilbey House (now Academic House) / Oval Road, Camden Town, London NW1 – Serge Chermayeff, 1937

Landfall / Crichel Mount Road, Poole, Dorset – Oliver Hill, 1938

Dunelm House / New Elvet, Durham, County Durham – Architects Co-Partnership, 1966

Canon (UK) Headquarters / Woodhatch, Cockshot Hill, Reigate, Surrey – David Richmond, 1999

BedZED / Wallington, South London – Bill Dunster, 2002

ALICE RAWSTHORN – design critic, author – alicerawsthorn.com
Design as an Attitude (2018)
Hello World: Where Design Meets Life (2013)

Keeling House / Claredale Street, Bethnal Green, London E2 – Denys Lasdun, 1955

Bernat Klein House / High Sunderland, Galashiels, Selkirk – Peter Womersley, 1957

Corner Green / Pond Road, Blackheath, London SE3 – Eric Lyons (Span Developments), 1959

Economist Plaza / St James's Street, London SW1 – Alison & Peter Smithson, 1964

Reliance Controls / Swindon, Wiltshire – Team 4, 1966

Alexandra & Ainsworth Estate / Camden, London NW8 – Neave Brown, 1978

Lloyd's Building / Lime Street, London EC3 – Richard Rogers Partnership, 1986

Idea Store Chrisp Street / Vesey Path, East India Dock Road, London E14 – David Adjaye, 2004

Hepworth Wakefield / Gallery Walk, Wakefield, West Yorkshire – David Chipperfield Architects, 2011

Kettle's Yard extensions / Castle Street, Cambridge –
Leslie Martin & David Owers, 1970
Jamie Fobert Architects, 2018

RICHARD ROGERS - Rogers Stirk Harbour + Partners - rsh-p.com
Must-see project: Lloyd's Building / Lime Street, London EC3, Richard Rogers Partnership, 1986

Crystal Palace / Hyde Park, London W2 (1851); then Sydenham Hill, London SE26 (1854-1936) – Joseph Paxton, 1851

Mackintosh building, Glasgow School of Art / Renfrew Street, Glasgow – Charles Rennie Mackintosh, 1909

Highpoint / North Hill, Highgate, London N6 – Berthold Lubetkin (Tecton), 1935 & 1938

Engineering Building, University of Leicester / University Road, Leicester, Leicestershire – James Stirling & James Gowan, 1963

Robin Hood Gardens / Woolmore Street, Poplar, London E14 – Alison & Peter Smithson, 1972 (demolished in 2019)

Sainsbury Centre for Visual Arts, University of East Anglia / Norfolk Road, Norwich, Norfolk – Foster Associates, 1978

The Shard / London Bridge Street, London SE1 – Renzo Piano Building Workshop, 2012

London Aquatics Centre / Olympic Park, London E20 – Zaha Hadid, 2011

Alton Estate / Roehampton, London SW15 – Rosemary Stjernstedt (LCC), 1958

Balfron Tower / St Leonards Road, Poplar, London E14 – Ernő Goldfinger, 1967

JONATHAN SERGISON – Sergison Bates architects – sergisonbates.com
Must-see project: Ruthin Craft Centre / Park Road, Ruthin, Denbighshire, Wales, 2009

Economist Plaza / St James's Street, London SW1 – Alison & Peter Smithson, 1964

Kettle's Yard extension / Castle Street, Cambridge – Leslie Martin & David Owers, 1970

The Sugden House / Devereux Drive, Watford, Hertfordshire – Alison & Peter Smithson, 1956

Red House / Tite Street, Chelsea, London SW3 – Tony Fretton Architects, 2001

The Lawns, Student Halls of Residence, University of Hull / Harland Way, Cottingham, East Yorkshire – Gillespie, Kidd & Coia, 1967

ANNE WARD - writer - ilike.org.uk
Way Out West: A Guide to the Hidden Joys of the West Country (2017)
Nothing To See Here: A Guide to the Hidden Joys of Scotland (2010)

A House for Essex / Black Boy Lane, Wrabness, Essex –
FAT Architecture & Grayson Perry, 2015

Barbican Estate / London EC2 –
Chamberlin, Powell and Bon, 1982

Royal Festival Hall, Southbank Centre / Belvedere Road, Lambeth, London SE1 – Robert Matthew & Leslie Martin, 1951

Liverpool Metropolitan Cathedral (Metropolitan Cathedral of Christ the King) / Mount Pleasant, Liverpool –
Frederick Gibberd, 1967

St Bride's Roman Catholic Church / Whitemoss Ave, East Kilbride, Glasgow – Gillespie, Kidd & Coia, 1964

Minack Theatre / Porthcurno, Penzance, Cornwall –
Rowena Cade, 1932

Preston Bus Station / Tithebarn Street, Preston, Lancashire –
Keith Ingham & Charles Wilson (BDP), 1969

Newcastle Civic Centre / Barras Bridge, Newcastle upon Tyne –
George Kenyon, 1967

Italian Chapel (Orkney POW Chapel) / Lamb Holm, Orkney –
Prisoners of War, 1945

Midland Hotel / Marine Road West, Morecambe, Lancashire – Oliver Hill, 1933

PETER YORK – author, broadcaster, cultural commentator
Dictators' Homes (2005)
Modern Times (1984)

Broadcasting House / Portland Place, London W1 – George Val Myer & F. J. Watson Hart, 1932

Arnos Grove Underground Station / Bowes Road, Arnos Grove, London N11 – Charles Holden, 1932

203-206 Piccadilly (Simpson's, now Waterstones) / London W1 – Joseph Emberton, 1936

New House / Arkwright Road, Hampstead, London NW3 – Samuel & Harding, 1939

76-78 Cambridge Street / Pimlico, London SW1 – Peter Foggo & David Thomas, 1969

Marine Court / Marina, St Leonards-on-Sea, East Sussex – Kenneth Dalgleish & Roger K. Pullen, 1938

Lillington Gardens Estate / Vauxhall Bridge Road, Pimlico, London SW1 – Darbourne & Darke, 1972

Highpoint / North Hill, Highgate, London N6 – Berthold Lubetkin (Tecton), 1935 & 1938

Gaumont State Cinema / Kilburn High Road, London NW6 – George Coles, 1937

Commonwealth Institute (original exterior) / Kensington High Street, London W8 – Robert Matthew, Johnson-Marshall and Partners, 1962

PAUL ZARA – Conran and Partners – conranandpartners.com
Must-see project: Refurbishment of Embassy Court / Kings Road, Hove, East Sussex (Wells Coates, 1935), Conran + Partners, 2006

De La Warr Pavilion / Marina, Bexhill-on-Sea, East Sussex – Erich Mendelsohn & Serge Chermayeff, 1936

High & Over / Highover Park, Amersham, Buckinghamshire – Amyas Connell, 1931

Highpoint I / North Hill, Highgate, London N6 – Berthold Lubetkin (Tecton), 1935

Highpoint II / North Hill, Highgate, London N6 – Berthold Lubetkin (Tecton), 1938

Isokon building (Lawn Road flats) / Lawn Road, Hampstead, London NW3 – Wells Coates, 1934

Embassy Court / Kings Road, Hove, East Sussex – Wells Coates, 1935

Royal Festival Hall, Southbank Centre / Belvedere Road, Lambeth, London SE1 – Robert Matthew & Leslie Martin, 1951

Lloyd's Building / Lime Street, London EC3 – Richard Rogers Partnership, 1986

Trellick Tower / Cheltenham Estate, Golborne Road, London W10 – Ernő Goldfinger, 1972

Economist Plaza / St James's Street, London SW1 – Alison & Peter Smithson, 1964

INDEX NAME OF THE ARCHITECT, ARTIST OR ARCHITECTURAL FIRM

PHOTO CREDITS

p. 13-89 + 117-119
© Grant Smith

EXCEPT FOR

p. 35 © Matthew Freedman

p. 41 © Simon Hart / Alamy Stock Photo

p. 69 © Sam Mellish

p. 79 © Peter Cook / VIEW

p. 11 © Alamy Stock Photo / The Print Collector

p. 91 © Kettle's Yard, University of Cambridge

p. 93 © Grant Smith / VIEW

p. 95 © Dennis Gilbert / VIEW

p. 97 © Jack Hobhouse

p. 99, 105 © Andy Stag / VIEW

p. 101 © Lin Gregory / Alamy Stock Photo

p. 103 © Peter Cook / VIEW

p. 107 © James Morris / VIEW

p. 109, 135 © Arcaid Images / Alamy Stock Photo

p. 111 © Dennis Gilbert / Ntpl / VIEW

p. 113 © Seier+Seier

p. 115 © Steve Cooper / Alamy Stock Photo

p. 121 © Iqbal Aalam

p. 123, 131 © David Borland / VIEW

p. 125 © James Brittain / VIEW

p. 127 © Amgueddfa Genedlaethol Cymru – National Museum of Wales

p. 129 © Coventry Cathedral

p. 133 © Quintin Lake

p. 137 © Chris Brink / VIEW

p. 139 © Gareth Gardner

p. 141 © University of Hull

p. 143-147 © Sally-Ann Norman / VIEW

p. 149 © Colin McLean / www.colinmcleanphotography.com

p. 151 © Marketing Edinburgh

p. 153 © VisitScotland / Kenny Lam

p. 155 © Dan Farrar / The National Churches Trust

p. 157 © John Maclean / VIEW

p. 159 © Tourism Northern Ireland

APPENDIX

p. 162 © The Modern House / **p. 163** © Landmark Trust / **p. 165** © Ned Trifle / **p. 166** © Gareth Williams / **p. 167** © Foster& Partners / **p. 169** © William Murphy / **p. 172** Steve Cadman **/ p. 173** Glasgow School of Art / **p. 176** © WowHaus / **p. 178** © Shutterstock / **p. 180** Caruso St John Architects / **p. 183** © RM Architects / **p. 185** © Eric Bjerke Sr. / **p. 187** © Bioregional – Tom Chance / **p. 188** © The Modern House / **p. 189** © Haworth Thompkins / **p. 190** © Tony Fretton Architects / **p. 192** © Steve Cadman / **p. 193** © WowHaus